Last Banjo in Paris

A COURTROOM COMEDY

by BARRY COOK

PBJ & BOOKS

© 2025 Studio PB&J, LLC

Published by PB&J Books
A division of Studio PB&J, LLC
1009 High Street, Paris, KY. 40361

This book is a work of fiction. Names, characters, places, and
incidents are either products of the author's imagination or are
used fictitiously and any resemblance to actual events or persons,
living or dead, is coincidental. Other than common spellcheck,
no AI generated text or images have been used to create this book.

ISBN: 979-8-9868895-3-5

For production inquires email: info@studiopbj.com
Professional and amateur productions are subject to a licensing
fee. Performance rights can be obtained from Studio PB&J, LLC.

Billing and credit requirements: If you have obtained
performance rights to this title, please refer to your licensing
agreement for important billing and credit requirements.

This play is dedicated to Stella Bell Birdwell

LAST BANJO IN PARIS

A Courtroom Comedy by Barry Cook

Setting: A Courtroom in Paris, Kentucky – 1974

Cast of Characters:

EDNA BUCHANAN
The Deceased Victim

MICHAEL P. NOLAN aka "MIKEY"
The Defendant - a Banjo Player

HORACE B. BIRDWEL
The Lawyer for the Defense

JESSICA LANTANA
State's Attorney - the Prosecutor

FRANKLIN WHEELHOUSE
The Honorable Judge

OFFICER MELVIN POTTER
The Court Bailiff

Witnesses for the Prosecution:

DEPUTY DARRYL MILES
First to Arrive at the Crime Scene

DR. LORETTA WILKINS
County Coroner - Expert Witness

DETECTIVE EUGENE FRICK
Kentucky DCI - Lead Detective

RAVI KOCHAR aka "COOKIE"
A Restaurateur

SAM WELLES
A Young Filmmaker

ANNABELLE ARBUCKLE
The Victim's Best Friend and Bookkeeper

Witnesses for the Defense:

ELBERT PACE aka "BERT"
An Elderly Barber

VINCENT CARNEY
A Fiddle Player - Bandmate of the Accused

SONJA GARCIA
Mandolin Player - Girlfriend of the Accused

BILLY MILLER
The Victim's Hired Hand

BEVERLY FRICK
Store Clerk - Wife of Detective Frick

Others in Court:

LUCY LUNGREN
Court Stenographer

ALICE RHODES
Birdwell's Legal Assistant

THE JURORS
Twelve Volunteers from the Audience

[ALL action takes place inside the Courtroom.]

ACT 1 / DAY 1

BOURBON COUNTY COURTHOUSE - PARIS
KENTUCKY - AUGUST 12TH, 1974

> *[**LUNGREN** enters carrying a Stenograph. She sets the machine on a tiny desk near the judge's bench, takes a seat then loudly cracks her knuckles—ready for work.]*

> *[POTTER enters and addresses all present:]*

POTTER: All rise. [pause as ALL rise] The Court of Bourbon County in the great Commonwealth of Kentucky is now in session.

> *[**LUNGREN** begins typing and continues throughout...]*

POTTER: All those having business before this Court shall be heard. The honorable Judge Franklin Wheelhouse presiding.

> *[Judge WHEELHOUSE enters from his chambers and takes his seat behind the bench.]*

POTTER: Please be seated.

WHEELHOUSE: Good morning. For the Court's record: Today is August 12th, 1974, Day 1 of the trial of The Commonwealth of Kentucky vs. Michael P. Nolan. Bailiff Potter, please bring in the Jurors.

[POTTER opens a door. Twelve volunteer JURORS from the audience enter and take their places.]

WHEELHOUSE: You may all be seated. [pause] Good morning, Jurors. Thank you for being here, then again, I don't reckon you had much choice in the matter. Nevertheless, my first task in every criminal trial is to give a few initial instructions to the jury. *[Refers to some written notes]* Each of you, as members of this jury, serves as a peer of the accused. Each of you is an equal member of this community, this commonwealth, and these United States. As citizens, you have rights—God given rights—that have been upheld by our legal system for many many years.

[Suddenly and with deft speed, WHEELHOUSE produces a fly swatter and slaps a fly on the bench then sweeps it off with the swatter.]

WHEELHOUSE: These flies sure love horse country in the middle of August. Where was I? *[refers back to his notes]* The accused perpetrator of the crime is only that— "accused." He too has all the rights that each of you possess. Including the right to a fair and speedy trial *and* the right to stand presumed innocent until proven guilty beyond a reasonable doubt. I will now ask the State to present its opening statement. Ms. Lantana, you may proceed.

[LANTANA, a smartly dressed woman in her early forties, approaches a podium facing the Jurors to deliver her opening statement.]

LANTANA: Thank you, Your Honor. Ladies and Gentlemen of the jury, You're about to hear stories, various stories—from members of Law Enforcement, from the County Coroner and other witnesses. As the State's Attorney for this case, it is my privilege to tell the first story. Mrs. Edna Buchanan's story.

[From behind the podium, LANTANA produces a large, printed photograph of eighty-something year old Mrs. Edna Buchanan posed smiling beside a horse. She holds the photo up for all to see.]

LANTANA: Mrs. Buchanan was an astute businesswoman, a pillar of this community. I wanted you all to see this beautiful photograph, so that you might keep her image in mind throughout this trial. Unfortunately, Mrs. Buchanan is not here to tell her own story. So, it's up to me.

[LANTANA sets aside the photo.]

LANTANA: Mrs. Edna Buchanan has been laid to rest beneath a willow tree just a mile south of this courthouse in Paris Memory Gardens. She lived a long life, a good life, but old age did not end her life. *[points at NOLAN]* He did. Michael P. Nolan, here wearing his Sunday best, praying that you will not believe Mrs. Buchanan's story. Particularly, the part where her life was cut short by Mr. Nolan on that chilly evening of March 16th of this year.

[WHEELHOUSE swats another fly.]

LANTANA: Next to Mr. Nolan is another man—the one who looks like he just stumbled out of an Agatha Christie novel. That man is the Defense Attorney for the accused. He will speak to you after I'm done. He'll likely tell you all about himself, then—he will also tell you a story, a fictional tale of a man wrongly accused. He'll also insist that Mrs. Buchanan's story, as I am about to tell it, is not the whole truth. Nevertheless, as the prosecutor in this case, I go first...

*[Stenographer **LUNGREN** cracks her knuckles again loudly.]*

LANTANA: On Saturday afternoon, March 16, Mrs. Buchanan was attending a musical event on the rooftop of the Beacon Building here in Paris. The music was being performed by a local Bluegrass ensemble known as the Bourbon String Busters. Mrs. Buchanan did not particularly care for Bluegrass music. However, she owned the three-story Beacon Building and had given her permission for the band to use its rooftop to film a performance of one of their tunes.

Shortly after the filming, as the members of the band were packing up, a single scream was heard. Followed by the awful—dreadful thud of a body hitting the sidewalk three stories below.

[WHEELHOUSE swats another fly.]

LANTANA: A second or two later, the elegant Royal Ascot hat, the same one Mrs. Buchanan is seen wearing here, *[holds up the photo again]* floated gently down and settled beside her lifeless body.

The evidence that will be presented to you during this trial will prove, beyond a reasonable doubt, that prior to Mrs. Buchanan's fall—in fact, the very cause of her fall—was due to Mrs. Buchanan being struck on the head with a blunt instrument. A blunt musical instrument. The very instrument that the defendant, *[gestures toward NOLAN]* Mr. Nolan, plucks as part of his livelihood. A five-string banjo!

I thank each and every one of you in advance for your attention and diligence in insuring that justice is delivered for Mrs. Edna Buchanan.

[LANTANA returns to her seat.]

WHEELHOUSE: Thank you, Ms. Lantana. The Defense may proceed with its opening statement, Mr. Birdwell...

> *[BIRDWELL, a man in his mid-sixties wearing*
> *a three-piece suit and an old, powdered*
> *barrister's wig, rises and takes his place at the*
> *podium to address the Jurors.]*

BIRDWELL: Good morning, Ladies and Gentlemen. There's lots of jokes about banjos and banjo players. Here's one: What do you call a banjo player wearing a nice suit? *[pause]* The Defendant.

> *[NOLAN stands, smiles, and opens his suit jacket to show its lining. WHEELHOUSE reprimands him:]*

WHEELHOUSE: The defendant will remain seated during opening statements.

> *[NOLAN buttons his jacket and sits.]*

BIRDWELL: Case in point. But this trial is no joke. As jurors, you have been gathered in this hallowed hall to perform a tremendous civic duty. This courtroom has seen hundreds, if not thousands, of trials over the years. Some say it is haunted by the ghosts of victims, judges, defendants, and attorneys that have passed on. Whether or not you believe that ghosts dwell in this courtroom is neither here nor there, but *one* thing is certain: The eyes of those who have gone before us *are* watching, to make sure we get this right. Which brings me to this... I'm sure you're all curious about it. *[BIRDWELL touches his wig.]* But my wig is also not a joke. Nor is it on my head as a fashion statement—unlike the hundred-dollar pair of Halston loafers that Ms. Lantana has worn to Court today.

> *[LANTANA wags her head.]*

BIRDWELL: No, I wear this wig as a reminder of my great-grandfather Lord Walter Birdwell. He was a barrister who proudly wore this wig while defending clients before the high courts of Great Britain. I wear it as a reminder of him and others who have gone to their final reward, including the late Mrs. Edna Buchanan. They are all watching.

The State has already reached their conclusion that Mrs. Buchanan was murdered. If that were true, I know she would expect you to ensure that justice is delivered. On the other hand, if Mrs. Buchanan's fall was an accident or, Lord forbid, a successful attempt to end her own life—I believe she would also expect that *truth* to rise from these proceedings.

> *[WHEELHOUSE raises a fly swatter ready to pounce—but his eye tracks the fly as it apparently takes flight to safety.]*

BIRDWELL: Ms. Lantana said that I would *likely* tell you a fictional tale of Mr. Nolan's innocence. I will not. The evidence in this case will separate fact from fiction. It is not my job to prove that Michael P. Nolan is innocent. As Judge Wheelhouse has stated, Mr. Nolan is presumed innocent until it is proven beyond *any* reasonable doubt that he had a hand in Mrs. Buchanan's fall from the roof. My job, as Defense Attorney, is to make sure that the Prosecuting Attorney, Ms. Lantana, does *her* job. The burden to prove my client's guilt, in this case, is hers alone. Folks, it is imperative that we get this right. Thank you kindly.

> *[BIRDWELL returns to his seat beside the defendant.]*

WHEELHOUSE: Ms. Lantana, are you ready to call your first witness?

> *[LANTANA stands.]*

LANTANA: Yes, Your Honor. The State calls Deputy Darryl Miles to the stand.

> *[MILES goes to the Witness Stand. POTTER approaches.]*

POTTER: Please raise your right hand. *[MILES does so.]* Do you solemnly swear that the testimony you are about to give is the truth, the whole truth and nothing but the truth, so help you God?

MILES: I do.

POTTER: Take a seat, Darryl.

[LANTANA approaches the witness.]

LANTANA: Good morning, Deputy Miles. Could you state your name and occupation for the Court?

MILES: Darryl Miles. I'm a deputy for the Bourbon County Sheriff's Department.

LANTANA: And how long have you held that position?

MILES: Four years and four months.

LANTANA: Deputy Miles, were you the first law enforcement officer to arrive at the scene of the Beacon Building on the afternoon of March 16th?

MILES: I was.

LANTANA: And what did you see?

MILES: The ambulance had just arrived. The attendants were checking on the condition of the deceased.

LANTANA: Are you stating that Mrs. Buchanan was already dead when you arrived?

MILES: As a doorknob.

LANTANA: No need for euphemisms, Deputy. A *yes* or *no* will suffice.

MILES: Yes.

LANTANA: Now, after you arrived and assessed the scene, what did you do next?

MILES: I taped off the area.

LANTANA: Taped off? What did you use to tape off the area?

MILES: You know, the yellow plastic tape that says, 'Crime Scene - Do Not Cross.'

LANTANA: So, you had determined that a crime had been committed—

[BIRDWELL lifts a hand.]

BIRDWELL: Objection, Your Honor. That's not a question...

WHEELHOUSE: Ms. Lantana, a question please.

LANTANA: By putting up the 'Crime Scene' tape, had you already determined that a crime had been committed at the scene?

MILES: No, ma'am. It was the only tape I had in the trunk of my patrol car.

LANTANA: I see. What happened next?

MILES: I radioed a call to the station, and the Coroner was dispatched to my location.

LANTANA: How long before the Coroner arrived?

MILES: Ten, maybe twelve minutes.

LANTANA: Thank you, Deputy Miles. *[Turns to the bench.]* No further questions, Your Honor.

> *[LANTANA returns to her seat at the prosecutor's table.]*

WHEELHOUSE: The Defense may now question the witness.

BIRDWELL: Thank you, Your Honor.

> *[BIRDWELL approaches Miles.]*

BIRDWELL: Good morning, Deputy.

MILES: Mornin.'

BIRDWELL: After the Coroner arrived on scene, did you go up to the rooftop of the Beacon Building?

MILES: Yes sir.

BIRDWELL: Can you tell us what you saw there?

MILES: Three people were on the roof. Sam Welles, Vincent Carney, and Michael Nolan.

BIRDWELL: Did you question those three individuals?

MILES: Only briefly.

BIRDWELL: And did you gather any evidence from the roof?

MILES: Yes. I collected one red high-heeled shoe, a left shoe, that matched one still on Mrs. Buchanan's right foot down below.

> *[BIRDWELL strolls to the evidence table and picks up the shoe.]*

BIRDWELL: This shoe?

MILES: Yep.

BIRDWELL: Were any other items collected?

MILES: It was almost dark. I decided to wrap things up and come back the following morning.

BIRDWELL: Did you leave the crime scene tape up overnight?

MILES: Yep. It was Saturday night. Lots of people were starting to line up to see the movie at the Strand.

BIRDWELL: So, the next morning you returned and collected more evidence?

MILES: Yep. I took down the crime scene tape. KDCI, State police, were already on the scene so I left and found Mr. Nolan at his apartment. That's when I collected the banjo as evidence. It wasn't till Tuesday that I got the processed film from the Welles boy's camera.

BIRDWELL: Why was the film collected?

MILES: I thought there was a good chance that Sammy Welles may have caught something with his camera... that might shed light on the case.

BIRDWELL: Back to Mr. Nolan. Did he surrender his banjo?

MILES: Well, he pulled his banjo case out from behind his sofa. I asked him to open it.

BIRDWELL: Was there a banjo inside the case?

MILES: Yep.

BIRDWELL: Could you please summarize the conversation you had with Mr. Nolan at that time?

MILES: Mr. Nolan seemed surprised—sorta confused. Said the banjo in his case was the 'prop banjo.'

BIRDWELL: Prop? What do you mean?

MILES: He explained that for the finale—of the thing they were filming—he had planned to smash a banjo. 'Course he didn't plan on smashing his good one, the one he normally plays. Said they had a cheap one, a prop to smash.

BIRDWELL: But was it smashed? The cheap one in his case? The prop banjo?

MILES: Nope. It was fully intact. They never filmed the finale. Sammy Welles, told me they were—what was it?—"Losing the light." Yeah, meaning the sun was going down. It was gettin' dark. So, they decided to film that part on another day.

BIRDWELL: I see. But did he also have his 'good' banjo?

MILES: Nope. Matter a fact, he seemed a bit panicked, started looking high and low for his good one. I helped him search, but it wasn't there in his apartment.

BIRDWELL: Did he oblige and let you take the cheap prop banjo?

MILES: He did.

BIRDWELL: Is that the banjo now in evidence? *[gestures toward the evidence table]* The one on that table yonder?

MILES: It is.

BIRDWELL: And you are aware that the State has asserted that a banjo was the murder weapon in this case?

MILES: I am.

BIRDWELL: Could you tell us about the rolls of film you collected?

MILES: Welles had dropped off his movie film at the Fotomat that Monday after the incident. I escorted him to pick up the processed film on Tuesday when it was ready.

BIRDWELL: And that film, subsequently, was also collected as evidence?

MILES: Yep. It was.

BIRDWELL: Finally, is it also *your* assertion, as a law enforcement officer, that a banjo was used to murder Mrs. Buchanan?

MILES: My job was to secure the scene, get initial witness statements and collect evidence. I'm not a detective.

BIRDWELL: So, you cannot testify with *certainty* that a banjo was used as a weapon in this case?

MILES: No, I cannot.

[BIRDWELL turns to the judge.]

BIRDWELL: No further questions, Your Honor.

WHEELHOUSE: You are dismissed, Deputy. You may leave the courtroom.

[MILES stands and exits]

WHEELHOUSE: Ms. Lantana, you may call your next witness.

LANTANA: Thank you, Your Honor. If it pleases the Court, the State calls Dr. Loretta Wilkins to the stand.

> *[WILKINS, a woman in her fifties, comes forward to be sworn in.]*

POTTER: Please raise your right hand. *[WILKINS complies.]* Do you solemnly swear that the testimony you are about to give is the truth, the whole truth and nothing but the truth, so help you God?

WILKINS: Yes, I do.

POTTER: Please be seated.

> *[LANTANA approaches the witness.]*

LANTANA: Good morning doctor. Would you please state your name for the record?

WILKINS: Dr. Loretta Wilkins.

LANTANA: Thank you, Dr. Wilkins. Would you please tell the Court your present occupation?

WILKINS: Yes. I'm employed as the Chief Medical Examiner for Bourbon County.

LANTANA: Will you share with the Court where you were educated and your work history?

WILKINS: Yes. I received my Doctorate in Forensic Pathology from Vanderbilt University in 1964. I practiced in Tennessee, in the Davidson County Morgue, for six years then took the job here in Bourbon County Kentucky where I currently practice.

LANTANA: Would you consider yourself an expert in the cause of a person's death?

WILKINS: Yes. With thorough examination of a deceased person's body, the cause of death can usually be determined.

LANTANA: When you arrived on the scene of Mrs. Buchanan's death. Did you determine that she was deceased?

WILKINS: Yes, it was quite apparent.

LANTANA: Once it was determined that Mrs. Buchanan was deceased, was her body removed from the scene and taken to the Medical Examiner's facility?

WILKINS: Yes, with the aid of my resident Dr. Morphew.

LANTANA: Did you perform an autopsy on the body of Mrs. Buchanan?

WILKINS: Yes. Anytime there is a death by accident, or any suspicious or unknown cause, it is a requirement from the Commonwealth that a complete autopsy be performed.

LANTANA: In layman's terms, could you share with the Court the findings of your medical examination of Mrs. Buchanan's body?

WILKINS: Yes. The autopsy was performed the morning of March 17th. We began our examination at about 7:10 am. The major injury to the body was a shattered cranium. Mrs. Buchanan also suffered multiple broken bones including a fractured left femur, a broken left arm, the ulna, plus multiple broken ribs.

LANTANA: Did you find any unusual injuries or injuries that did not seem to match what you would expect to find on a person that had simply fallen thirty feet to a concrete sidewalk?

WILKINS: Not initially. But as I examined the back of the decedent's head closely, I saw what appeared to be some unusual marks and a laceration that were not consistent with her other injuries.

LANTANA: Could you describe those "unusual" marks and the laceration to the back of Mrs. Buchanan's scalp?

WILKINS: Yes. The laceration was in the shape of a crescent moon. Along its outer curve, there were three small round bruises—like planets orbiting the crescent.

[LANTANA turns to the judge.]

LANTANA: Your honor, the State wishes to enter exhibits C-01 and C-06 into evidence at this time.

WHEELHOUSE: You may. Bailiff Potter, if you'd please dim the lights.

> *[POTTER dims the lights in the courtroom. LANTANA crosses to a carousel slide projector aimed at a freestanding retractable movie screen. She flips a switch. An image appears.]*

LANTANA: Did you make the drawing and notes we now see on this slide Dr. Wilkins?

WILKINS: Yes. That's my initial notation of the wounds I found on the posterior of the decedent's scalp. We also have photographs of the injuries—

LANTANA: We'll spare the Court those photographs for the time being. Did these unusual injuries cause you to determine that Mrs. Buchanan's death was not an accident?

WILKINS: The cause of her death was blunt force trauma to the skull, which happened instantaneously when Mrs. Buchanan's head came in contact with the sidewalk. The marks to the back of her scalp would *not* have caused her death. This led me to the conclusion that an object struck the back of Mrs. Buchanan's head prior to her fall. Given the order in which these injuries occurred, it indicated that Mrs. Buchanan received an initial blow to the back of the head—and that blow may have been the catalyst of her fall from the rooftop, the reason she fell.

LANTANA: And this object that left those unusual marks and crescent-moon-shaped laceration to the back of the scalp—did you determine, could you determine, what left those marks?

WILKINS: It took a while, but I was eventually able to match those injuries to the tension hoop and brackets common to a banjo.

LANTANA: You did say, "a banjo"?

WILKINS: Yes, a banjo. The musical instrument.

[BIRDWELL jumps to his feet—]

BIRDWELL: Objection! This is pure speculation.

WHEELHOUSE: The expert is entitled to offer her opinion. Overruled.

LANTANA: *[Addressing Wilkins]* And, how did you reach your conclusion?

WILKINS: The only reason I considered the instrument as a factor was at the suggestion of Dr. Earl Morphew, who assisted me in the autopsy.

LANTANA: How did Dr. Morphew connect the dots?

WILKINS: He told me about a Christmas morning when he was a child. He had kicked a hole through his younger brother's gift, a banjo. All Earl got that Christmas was a tangerine and a kazoo. Guess he was jealous.

[Laughter arises from the gallery.]

WHEELHOUSE: Please just answer the questions, Dr. Wilkins.

[WILKINS nods.]

LANTANA: So, Dr. Morphew's familiarity with banjos helped you make the connection?

WILKINS: That's correct. It would have never crossed my mind otherwise.

> *[LANTANA returns to the slide projector, grabs the tethered hand-held remote and gives it a click, advancing the carousel to the next slide showing details of a banjo's tension hoop and brackets.]*

LANTANA: Can you please describe this slide?

WILKINS: Yes, that's a photo of a banjo's tension hoop and brackets.

> *[LANTANA 'clicks' back and forth between the two slides to compare Wilkin's drawing of the injury with the banjo photo.]*

LANTANA: Is that the banjo the Sheriff's department collected as evidence in this case?

WILKINS: I'm not sure where that photo originated. I think it's just a generic banjo. I had no knowledge of what evidence had been collected, at that particular time.

LANTANA: So, on the basis of the autopsy and your consultation with Dr. Morphew, you concluded that Mrs. Buchanan did not accidentally fall, or purposefully jump, from the roof of the Beacon Building. Correct?

> *[BIRDWELL stands.]*

BIRDWELL: Objection. She's leading the witness.

WHEELHOUSE: Please rephrase your question, Ms. Lantana.

> *[BIRDWELL sits.]*

LANTANA: Of course, Your Honor. *[Turns to the witness]* In your *professional* opinion, did Mrs. Buchanan accidentally fall or purposefully jump from the rooftop?

WILKINS: The blow from the banjo either knocked her off her feet, which resulted in her fall, or the blow knocked her unconscious, causing her to fall. That's my opinion.

LANTANA: Thank you doctor. *[Turns to the judge]* No further questions, Your Honor.

WHEELHOUSE: Thank you. *[pause]* Mr. Birdwell, do you wish to question the witness?

> *[BIRDWELL stands as LANTANA takes her seat.]*

> *[**LUNGREN** cracks her knuckles again.]*

BIRDWELL: I do, Your Honor. *[He approaches the witness.]* Good morning, Dr. Wilkins.

WILKINS: Good morning, Horace.

BIRDWELL: I haven't seen you since the Goodlette case. How *have* you been?

WILKINS: Busy. Death never takes a day off.

BIRDWELL: It surely does not. I admire what you do Loretta. Not many people are fit for a job in the morgue.

WHEELHOUSE: Please ask a question Mr. Birdwell.

BIRDWELL: Yes sir. *[pause]* Dr. Wilkins, As someone who deals with death on a daily basis, would you consider Mrs. Buchanan's autopsy a routine one?

WILKINS: I'd say more complex than most. There were a lot of pieces to put together—if you catch my drift.

BIRDWELL: I do. Now, you've just testified that you believe a banjo was *[Twirls his wrist with index finger pointed.]* somehow involved in the death of Mrs. Buchanan. Do I have that right?

WILKINS: You do.

BIRDWELL: A Banjo. Like what J.D. Crowe plays?

WILKINS: I'm not familiar with that individual.

BIRDWELL: Well then, how about the defendant? Are you aware that Mr. Nolan plays the banjo?

WILKINS: I've been informed.

BIRDWELL: And you've testified that a blow from a banjo caused Mrs. Buchanan to fall from the roof. Is *that* correct?

WILKINS: I think I said, it *may* have. I believe it did. That's my opinion.

BIRDWELL: So, there *is* the possibility that something other than a banjo's tension hoop and its brackets struck the back of Mrs. Buchanan's head prior to her fall?

WILKINS: If there's a better explanation, I'm eager to hear it.

BIRDWELL: Thank you, Dr. Wilkins. *[Addresses the Bench]* No further questions Your Honor but the Defense requests that the witness remain on call.

> *[BIRDWELL returns to the Defense table and sits.]*

WHEELHOUSE: Duly noted. Dr. Wilkins, you are dismissed. You may call your next witness Ms. Lantana.

> *[WILKINS leaves the stand and exits. LANTANA stands.]*

LANTANA: Thank you, Judge. The state calls Detective Eugene Frick to the stand.

> *[FRICK, a tall, handsome man in his mid-thirties wearing a nice suit enters the courtroom and takes the stand.]*

POTTER: Please raise your right hand. *[Frick complies]* Do you solemnly swear that the testimony you are about to give is the truth, the whole truth and nothing but the truth, so help you God?

FRICK: *[Smiles]* I do.

POTTER: Please take a seat.

[LANTANA approaches Frick.]

LANTANA: Good afternoon, Detective. Could you please state your name and occupation for the Court?

FRICK: Detective Eugene Frick. I'm a homicide detective with KDCI.

LANTANA: That's the Kentucky Department of Criminal Investigation, correct?

FRICK: Yes, ma'am.

> *[**LUNGREN** hangs on Frick's every word. She seems enamored with him.]*

LANTANA: Why were *you* assigned as Lead Detective for this case?

FRICK: I'm the only homicide detective in the department residing in Bourbon County. My superiors saw it as a good fit.

LANTANA: And when were you assigned to the case?

FRICK: After the Coroner completed her autopsy.

LANTANA: The same day? March 17th?

FRICK: *[Pauses to search his mind.]* I believe the day after. Yes. The day after the autopsy, Monday the 18th.

LANTANA: *What* was the first order of business in your investigation?

FRICK: I made contact with the Sheriff's Department to inform them that I would be taking over the case as a murder investigation. I was put in touch with Deputy Miles who took me through the evidence that had been collected. He then escorted me to the crime scene to have a look.

LANTANA: Did you gather additional evidence at the scene?

FRICK: No additional physical evidence, but I took numerous photos at street level and some from the roof of the Beacon Building.

LANTANA: Was there a KDCI photographer with you?

FRICK: *[Flashes a smile]* No, ma'am, our budgets are tight. Photography happens to be my hobby. I'm fairly accomplished. I took the pictures.

LANTANA: The State would like to enter these photos as State's evidence S-04 and S-05.

WHEELHOUSE: Duly noted. Please proceed.

> *[WHEELHOUSE nods to Potter. POTTER switches off the overhead lights in the courtroom.]*

> *[LANTANA moves to the slide projector and clicks to the next slide.]*

LANTANA: Thank you. Detective Frick, could you please describe the slide on the screen?

FRICK: Yes, that is a photo of the three-story Beacon building from street level.

> *[LANTANA clicks to the next slide.]*

LANTANA: And this one?

FRICK: That shows the general layout of the rooftop. The ventilation pipes and the door that provides roof access.

LANTANA: So, that small structure, similar in size and shape to say, an outhouse—with a single door, is the only way to and from the roof top?

FRICK: Well unfortunately, Mrs. Buchanan left the roof in a different manner.

LANTANA: Of course. Which brings us to this photo...

> *[LANTANA clicks to the next slide.]*

LANTANA: Could you please describe it for the Court?

FRICK: I took that from the rooftop. The outline on the sidewalk marks the position where the victim's body was found.

LANTANA: Did you outline the body?

FRICK: No, as I mentioned, I was assigned *after* the Coroner's Office made its report. Deputy Miles traced her outline.

LANTANA: Could you please describe this next photo?

> *[LANTANA clicks to the next slide. It's a picture of Detective Frick's dog, a German Shepherd.]*

FRICK: Whoops. *[chuckles]* Sorry, that wasn't supposed to be in there. That's my dog Shep.

> *[LANTANA clicks the next slide. It's a picture of a banjo.]*

LANTANA: Let's try this one.

FRICK: There we go. That's the banjo.

> *[LANTANA turns off the slide projector then goes to the evidence table and picks up the banjo. POTTER raises the lights.]*

LANTANA: Gee, *this thing is heavy.* Detective Frick, do you recognize this instrument?

FRICK: Yes, the same one in the photo, the banjo collected into evidence by Deputy Miles.

LANTANA: In light of Dr. Wilkin's initial observations during the autopsy, and her conclusion that Mrs. Buchanan's head had been struck by a banjo, did you confirm that the County Coroner had gotten it right?

FRICK: I took the banjo to the morgue and personally compared its tension hoop and brackets to the marks on the back of the victim's skull. *[Looks at Jurors]* They matched.

LANTANA: Was the banjo tested for blood residue?

FRICK: Yes.

LANTANA: Was there blood on the banjo?

FRICK: There were several small traces that tested as blood. The same blood type as Mrs. Buchanan.

LANTANA: Were you able to question Mr. Nolan about his whereabouts and actions on the afternoon of March 16th?

FRICK: Yes, Mr. Nolan was brought in for an interview the day after I visited the morgue.

LANTANA: In your own words, could you summarize that conversation?

FRICK: *[Addresses the Jurors]* I interviewed Mr. Nolan, here at the Sheriff's department, downstairs in this courthouse, on March 18th at about 4pm. Mr. Nolan was nervous and denied any part in Mrs. Buchanan's fall from the roof. He claimed *[smiles broadly]* that he and his girlfriend were engaged in an argument just prior to the moment Mrs. Buchanan fell. He said a stiff breeze had blown Mrs. Buchanan's hat from her head, that she had reached to grab it, had stumbled—and fell off the roof.

LANTANA: Did you believe his story?

FRICK: His version of events did not line up with the physical evidence.

LANTANA: Did you interview other members of the band?

FRICK: Yes. I interviewed the other four band members... *[FRICK pulls a small notepad from his inside jacket pocket and opens it and reads.]* They were Sonja Garcia, Vincent Carney, Greg Jarrett, and Danny Boyd.

> *[From his seat at the Defense table, NOLAN begins singing...]*

NOLAN: *[Sings to the tune of "Danny Boy"]* O' Danny Boyd, the pipes the pipes are ca-all-ling...

> *[Laughter erupts from the gallery. WHEELHOUSE bangs his gavel.]*

WHEELHOUSE: Order in this Court! Order! Order.

> *[The laughter subsides...]*

WHEELHOUSE: I warn the defendant that I will find him in contempt if he speaks—or sings again, without being asked to do so.

> *[BIRDWELL can't contain his grin. He elbow-nudges Nolan.]*

WHEELHOUSE: You may proceed, Ms. Lantana.

LANTANA: Thank you. Detective, would you please continue your summary of the additional interviews?

FRICK: *[Continues from his notes]* Yes, I questioned Greg Jarrett, who played the upright bass, and Danny Boyd, *[Frick shoots a threatening eye toward the defendant.]* the guitar player for the band. Both had left the scene about ten minutes prior to Mrs. Buchanan's fall. I was later able to verify both their alibis. Sonja Garcia, who played mandolin and identified herself as Mr. Nolan's *ex*-girlfriend, confirmed that she and the defendant had an argument but stated she had left the rooftop by way of the stairs prior to Mrs. Buchanan's fall. Vincent Carney, the fiddler in the outfit, said he was putting away his instrument and his back was turned to Mrs. Buchanan when she fell from the roof. Mr. Carney was, however, the *first* person to look over the roof ledge and see Mrs. Buchanan's lifeless body on the sidewalk below. And I questioned Sam Welles, the young man with the movie camera. He also heard the scream and filmed the aftermath of Mrs. Buchanan's body on the sidewalk.

LANTANA: Thank you, Detective. No further questions, Your Honor.

[LANTANA moves to her seat.]

WHEELHOUSE: Mr. Birdwell, your witness.

[BIRDWELL stands and approaches the witness.]

BIRDWELL: Good afternoon, Detective. Prior to Mrs. Buchanan's untimely demise, did you ever visit the Beacon Building?

FRICK: Fairly often.

BIRDWELL: Why's that?

FRICK: My wife Beverly works there. In the Sears store on the ground floor.

BIRDWELL: So, did you perceive any 'conflict of interest' due to your wife's employment at the crime scene?

FRICK: It's only coincidental. My superiors didn't have a problem assigning me to the case.

BIRDWELL: Thought I'd ask. Coincidences always concern me in criminal cases. Now, as for the interrogations you conducted—

[LANTANA interrupts.]

LANTANA: Objection! Mr. Birdwell cannot imply that the *interviews* conducted by Detective Frick were interrogations.

WHEELHOUSE: Sustained. Mr. Birdwell, please refrain from characterizing the interviews as interrogations.

BIRDWELL: Apologies, Your Honor. Detective Frick, when you questioned Ms. Garcia—when she told you she and Mr. Nolan were having a spat—did she say she saw him take his anger out on Mrs. Buchanan with his banjo?

> *[NOLAN licks his forefinger and pantomimes 'chalking one up' for the defendant. WHEELHOUSE sees him and slaps the bench with his flyswatter.]*

WHEELHOUSE: Mr. Nolan, you'll refrain from comment—spoken or otherwise. Is that understood?

> *[NOLAN pantomimes zipping his lips.]*

WHEELHOUSE: You may continue your cross-examination, Mr. Birdwell.

BIRDWELL: Thank you, Judge. So, did Ms. Garcia see Mr. Nolan whack Mrs. Buchanan upside the head with a banjo?

FRICK: No. She swore that Mr. Nolan could not have knocked Mrs. Buchanan off the roof.

BIRDWELL: But you did *not* believe her?

FRICK: No... because if she had already left by way of the stairs, she had no way of knowing what Mr. Nolan did or did not do after that. This is fairly typical, nine times out of ten, a spouse or romantic partner will try to protect the one they love.

BIRDWELL: But did you not *just testify* that she referred to Mr. Nolan as her *ex-boyfriend*?

FRICK: At the time of the incident, they were still a couple. When I interviewed her, she expressed regret for breaking up with Mr. Nolan.

BIRDWELL: A yes or no will do. Now, about the fiddle player, did Vincent Carney confess anything to you during his interview?

FRICK: Yes. *[Rolls his eyes]* He claimed that he and Billy Miller had stolen Mr. Nolan's banjo that afternoon.

BIRDWELL: Whoa! Hang on. This is quite a revelation. So why didn't Mr. Carney become a suspect in your investigation?

FRICK: For the simple fact that Mr. Nolan's banjo was found, in Mr. Nolan's possession, behind the sofa in his apartment.

BIRDWELL: Are you aware that Mr. Nolan told Deputy Miles that the banjo found behind his sofa was not his but instead a prop for the film?

FRICK: Well, yes, I was aware of Mr. Nolan's claim. He repeated that several times during our interview. And I heard Mr. Carney's confession firsthand, but the facts didn't support their stories. Friends, like lovers, are also likely to offer alternate theories or stories to help their buddies avoid prosecution, even if it means they themselves could be implicated in a lesser crime. I've seen it a hundred times.

BIRDWELL: So, there *is* a possibility, even a remote one, that this banjo—collected into evidence... *[BIRDWELL picks up the banjo from the evidence table and holds it throughout this line of questioning (perhaps even strumming it a time or two for emphasis).]* This banjo *(strum...)* was *not* the one Mr. Nolan played during the filming of the band's performance on March 16th? Did you bother to compare this banjo to the one being played in the film from Sam Welles movie camera? *(strum...)*

FRICK: I did. The banjo in the filmed footage looked the same to me.

BIRDWELL: Are you an expert on banjo makes and models?

FRICK: No, I'm not. But the fact that Mr. Nolan's prints and Mrs. Buchanan's blood were found on that instrument provided sufficient evidence to go to the District Attorney for an arrest warrant.

BIRDWELL: Did you ever consider that Mr. Nolan's prints were on this instrument because he lifted it out of the case, in Deputy Miles' presence, the moment he recognized it wasn't his?

FRICK: *[Growing bothered, his anger flashes.]* Look, for all I know, Mr. Nolan may own a dozen banjos—all with his greasy prints on them.

BIRDWELL: And the blood. Was its type consistent with Mrs. Buchanan's?

FRICK: Yes, O Negative. Only thirteen percent of people have that.

BIRDWELL: You are aware that Mr. Nolan is related to Mrs. Buchanan. Perhaps they share the same blood type. Did you test Mr. Nolan's blood type?

[FRICK hesitates...]

BIRDWELL: Yes or No, Detective Frick?

FRICK: No.

BIRDWELL: Now, you just testified that you took *this* banjo, collected by Deputy Miles, to the morgue to compare it with the wounds on the victim's scalp. Correct?

FRICK: Yes.

BIRDWELL: So, is it possible that during your comparison, Mrs. Buchanan's blood could have been transferred to this banjo?

FRICK: Not possible. That would imply sloppy work on my part.

BIRDWELL: Or maybe a precise piece of work to plant evidence against the defendant. Isn't that possible?

[LANTANA jumps to her feet.]

LANTANA: Objection! Counsel is making accusations against the witness!

WHEELHOUSE: Objection overruled. You may answer the question, Detective.

FRICK: Altering evidence, in any form, is a crime. I'm *not* the criminal in this case.

BIRDWELL: No further questions.

> *[BIRDWELL returns the banjo to the Evidence Table.]*

WHEELHOUSE: You may step down, Detective.

> *[FRICK exits the courtroom.]*

WHEELHOUSE: The State may call its next witness.

LANTANA: Thank you, Judge. The Prosecution calls Mr. Ravi Kochar to the stand.

> *[KOCHAR, a slight man in his thirties, enters and proceeds to the witness stand.]*

POTTER: Please raise your right hand. *[KOCHAR does]* Do you hereby swear that the testimony you are about to give is the truth, the whole truth and nothing but the truth—so help you God?

KOCHAR: Which god are we talking about?

[POTTER looks to the judge for guidance. WHEELHOUSE shrugs with raised palms.]

POTTER: Be seated.

[KOCHAR sits. LANTANA approaches]

LANTANA: Good Morning, Mr. Kochar.

KOCHAR: Namaste. Good morning.

LANTANA: Could you please state your name for the record?

KOCHAR: Ravi Kochar.

LANTANA: And what is your occupation sir?

KOCHAR: I'm the proprietor of Cookie's Burgers here in Paris.

LANTANA: Where is your restaurant located?

KOCHAR: On the corner of 8th and Main, next to Strand —the movie theater—right across from the Beacon Building.

LANTANA: The Beacon Building. Also known as the 'tallest three-story building' in the world?

KOCHAR: *[chuckles]* Yes, that's what I've heard. Out-of-towners think so. They take pictures of it.

LANTANA: Would you please tell the Court what you saw in the late afternoon of March 16th?

KOCHAR: Yes. I was wiping down the counter, facing the windows where the booths are. My eye caught sight of something, *[He gets emotional.]* something falling... from the roof across the street.

[KOCHAR struggles to hold back tears.]

LANTANA: Take your time, Mr. Kochar.

KOCHAR: Then I saw Bert, the barber, standing on the corner with his hands over his eyes. I ran out to see what had happened. I'd hoped that someone had just dropped a bucket of paint...or something... but then I saw... it was... it was terrible.

LANTANA: Did you call for help?

KOCHAR: Yes. I keep the number by my phone, you know in case someone chokes or something. I hurried back inside and called for the ambulance.

LANTANA: How long before they arrived?

KOCHAR: Maybe three, four minutes.

LANTANA: Did you see a red pickup truck pull away from the curb around the time Mrs. Buchanan fell from the roof?

KOCHAR: I don't remember that. But Billy Miller had just stopped in for a Coke. I think he drives a red truck.

LANTANA: Did any of the band members eat at your restaurant that day?

KOCHAR: Yes, the entire band had lunch with me. I was super busy between noon and two.

LANTANA: Did you notice anything unusual about Mr. Nolan's demeanor, the way he was acting?

KOCHAR: His aura was off. He likes to, how do you say?... 'play a fool' to make people laugh. But he was *so* quiet that day.

LANTANA: As if maybe, something was on his mind?

[BIRDWELL interrupts.]

BIRDWELL: Objection. Innuendo.

WHEELHOUSE: I'll allow it. Please answer the question, Mr. Kochar.

KOCHAR: Yes. He seemed in his own world, until Beverly came in to pick up a 'to-go' order.

LANTANA: Beverly Frick?

KOCHAR: Yes, from the Sears store.

LANTANA: So, what changed, in Mr. Nolan's demeanor, when Mrs. Frick came in?

KOCHAR: He spilled his milkshake.

LANTANA: Was there anything else about Mr. Nolan's behavior that seemed odd that day?

KOCHAR: He didn't finish his burger.

LANTANA: Did Mrs. Buchanan eat lunch at your establishment that day?

KOCHAR: No. Not that day.

LANTANA: Thank you, Mr. Kochar. No further questions your honor.

WHEELHOUSE: Would the Defense like to question Mr. Kochar?

BIRDWELL: Indeed, Your Honor.

[BIRDWELL approaches the witness.]

BIRDWELL: Mr. Kochar, do your customers call you "Cookie"?

KOCHAR: Yes, most everyone. *[chuckles]* I like it.

BIRDWELL: Na-mas-tay, Cookie.

KOCHAR: *[putting on his best Kentucky accent]* Howdy, Horace.

BIRDWELL: *[chuckles]* Mr. Kochar. Did you see anything unusual during the time you and Bert were waiting for help to arrive?

KOCHAR: People may call me crazy but... I swear I saw Mrs. Buchanan's spirit rise up from her body and drift up Main street.

BIRDWELL: You saw her ghost?

KOCHAR: Yes, in Hindi we call it bhuta-ganan.

BIRDWELL: So, you still practice Hinduism?

KOCHAR: No, I'm not so religious now. You know, burgers and all *[embarrassed chuckle]*.

BIRDWELL: Yes, understood. Now, did Mr. Nolan and Beverly Frick ever dine *together* at your place?

KOCHAR: No. Beverly always came in alone, just to pick up her lunch. Mikey and Sonja always shared a booth.

BIRDWELL: Is that Sonja Garcia, Mikey's bandmate?

KOCHAR: I think they're more than bandmates, but yes.

BIRDWELL: Are you aware that Ms. Garcia has been called to testify in this trial?

KOCHAR: Really? I mean, no I did not know that.

BIRDWELL: Would you call Mrs. Buchanan a regular customer at your establishment?

KOCHAR: No, she only stopped in for pie and coffee from time to time, but I wouldn't say she's a regular customer.

BIRDWELL: Did Mrs. Buchanan own the building where your hamburger stand is located?

KOCHAR: Yes, she did. The movie house too.

BIRDWELL: Was she a good landlady?

KOCHAR: Well, *[pause]* she was a good businesswoman.

BIRDWELL: Did she treat you fairly, as a Tenant?

KOCHAR: The rent's not cheap but the location is good. I'm able to earn a living making burgers.

BIRDWELL: And may I say, they're the best burgers this side of Frankfort! No further questions, Your Honor.

WHEELHOUSE: I'll need to ask the Jurors to disregard Mr. Birdwell's love of Cookie's burgers. However, talk of food reminds me that we should take a break for lunch. Is Cookie's open for lunch today, Mr. Kochar?

KOCHAR: We are, Your Honor.

WHEELHOUSE: You may step down, Mr. Kochar. *[lowers his voice]* Would you mind sending me over an order of Chili Fries?

KOCHAR: You got it, Judge.

>*[KOCHAR leaves the stand and exits the courtroom.]*

WHEELHOUSE: Court will be in recess for lunch until one o'clock.

>*[WHEELHOUSE strikes his gavel.]*

(Lights out)

(Lights up on:)

>*[ALL are in their respective places; Judge WHEELHOUSE is wiping his mouth and fingers with a paper napkin.]*

WHEELHOUSE: Ms. Lantana, *[burps]* you may call your next witness.

LANTANA: Thank you, Judge. The State calls Sam Welles to the stand.

>*[WELLES, a slim, long-haired boy of about fifteen enters the courtroom and proceeds to the witness stand.]*

POTTER: Please raise your right hand. *[WELLES complies.]* Do you hereby swear that the testimony you are about to give is the truth, the whole truth and nothing but the truth—so help you God?

WELLES: I do.

POTTER: Please be seated.

[LANTANA approaches the witness.]

LANTANA: Mr. Welles, are you presently a student at Bourbon County High School?

WELLES: You don't need to call me mister, but yes ma'am, I'll be a Junior next year.

LANTANA: What were you doing on the roof of the Beacon Building on the afternoon of March 16th of this year?

WELLES: I was filming the bluegrass band. They wanted to do something that looked like the Beatles playing *Get Back*. *[looks up]* You know, on a roof.

LANTANA: And the band you filmed was the Bourbon String Busters?

WELLES: Right, Mikey and them. Greg even wore a red raincoat like Ringo's. Did you know Ringo borrowed that raincoat from his girlfriend Barbara Hershey?

LANTANA: No. But back to the String Busters; Which of the band members approached you with the idea of filming the band?

WELLES: Mikey Nolan. [looks toward Nolan]. Hi Mikey. I met him at a party last fall where I showed a film that I'd made called "*Western Beef.*" He thought it was pretty cool, I guess.

[NOLAN gives a 'thumbs up.']

LANTANA: How did the filming go?

WELLES: Well, it's no "Fist Full of Dollars" but—

LANTANA: I was referring to the filming of the Bourbon String Busters.

WELLES: Oh. That was great, fine... until... you know.

LANTANA: Until Mrs. Buchanan's fall?

WELLES: That was nuts! At first the guys thought I'd pulled some sorta prank with a dummy. We did have a cowboy fall off the saloon roof in my western.

LANTANA: So, you did not see *or film* her fall?

WELLES: I was done filming the band for the day. I was using up my last bit of film on a shot of the sunset. When I heard the scream, I stopped the camera. When I turned 'round in that direction. I saw Vinny looking down over the side of the building. Mikey hurried over there too, to see what happened. Then I looked over the side.

LANTANA: Did you get any film of Mrs. Buchanan's body on the sidewalk below?

WELLES: Some. It turned out sorta dark on account of the sun going down.

LANTANA*: [Addresses the judge]* If it pleases the Court, the state would like to show that roll of film—from Mr. Welles' camera labeled State's exhibit F-03.

WHEELHOUSE: You may. I will advise those in the gallery and the Jurors that the film may be somewhat disturbing. Bailiff Potter, if you'd please dim the lights.

>*[POTTER dims the lights in the courtroom. LANTANA crosses to a Super 8 film projector atop an AV stand aimed at the movie screen. She flips a switch and the film rolls. The first few shots are of the band performing.]*

LANTANA: Mr. Welles, as the film plays, could you please describe what we're seeing on the screen?

WELLES: Yeah—there's the band playing. There's no sound because we recorded that earlier. I use my cassette deck, for 'playback,' so the band can play along with it. I put the sound and picture together later, in the edit, so it all syncs up in the end. Those are some close ups I did of their hands and stuff. *[pause]* There's some of the buildings around town. The top of the courthouse we're in right now... *[pauses to think about the irony]* freaky. There's the sun goin' down—nice. And that... that's poor Mrs. B. on the sidewalk. *[pause]* Oh, and that's a close up of her shoe still on the roof. I grabbed a quick shot of that—kinda dark.

> *[The shot taken from the rooftop showing the body on the sidewalk also shows a red truck pulling away from the curb. After the close up of the shoe, the film runs out. The screen goes bright white. POTTER turns the lights back on in the courtroom. LANTANA switches off the film projector.]*

LANTANA: Do you know *whose* truck that was, pulling away from the curb?

WELLES: I've seen it around, but I don't know who drives it.

LANTANA*: [Turns to the Bench]* No further questions, Your Honor.

> *[LANTANA returns to her seat .]*

WHEELHOUSE: Mr. Birdwell, do you have any questions for this witness?

BIRDWELL: Yes, Your Honor. *[Stands and approaches the witness.]* Good morning, Mr. Welles.

WELLES: Hello.

BIRDWELL: Do you know anything about a second banjo that was to be used on the day you filmed the band?

WELLES: Yeah. A prop banjo. A cheap one. Mikey was supposed to smash it like Hendrix as the film's finale.

BIRDWELL: Did he? Smash it?

WELLES: No. Like I said, we were losing the light. You know, it was gettin' dark. I talked to Mikey, and we decided to shoot it later as a 'pick up.'

BIRDWELL: A pickup?

WELLES: Yeah, we decided to shoot the banjo smashing later—pick up the filming on a different day.

BIRDWELL: I see. What happened to that prop banjo?

WELLES: I couldn't tell ya. I think Greg brought it. He may have left with it. I don't remember.

BIRDWELL: But you did see two banjos that day, correct?

WELLES: Mikey had his nice banjo with him that day but he used the prop for the filming so it would match when it came time to smash it. It didn't matter what the prop banjo sounded like since the tune they were playin' along with had already been recorded.

BIRDWELL: Fine. Let's get back to Mrs. Buchanan. Do you think a person would, or could, *scream* after being struck on the back of the head with a banjo?

[LANTANA rises.]

LANTANA: Objection! The witness is being asked to speculate.

WHEELHOUSE: Sustained. The question will be stricken from the record. Jurors will disregard.

BIRDWELL: *[addressing Welles]* Did you hear a scream?

WELLES: Sure did.

BIRDWELL: And what was it that made you want to capture that final closeup of Mrs. Buchanan's shoe?

WELLES: I guess it said a lot. You know, about what happened. Her dead body on the sidewalk, her left shoe still on the roof. Sorta poignant if you catch my drift.

BIRDWELL: Poignant... Thank you. *[Turns to bench]* No further questions.

WHEELHOUSE: You may step down, son.

> *[WELLES leaves the stand and exits the courtroom.]*

WHEELHOUSE: The State may call its next witness.

LANTANA: The State calls Annabelle Arbuckle to the stand.

> *[ARBUCKLE, a prim lady in her early seventies, enters to take the oath.]*

POTTER: Please raise your right hand. *[ARBUCKLE raises her hand.]* Do you solemnly swear that the testimony you are about to give is the truth, the whole truth and nothing but the truth, so help you God?

ARBUCKLE: I do.

POTTER: Please be seated.

LANTANA: Good afternoon, ma'am. Would you please state your name and occupation for the Court?

ARBUCKLE: Yes. I'm Annabelle Arbuckle. I worked thirty-six years as Mrs. Buchanan's bookkeeper.

LANTANA: Was she a good employer?

ARBUCKLE: She was wonderful... *[ARBUCKLE starts to get emotional...]* Edna was my best friend.

> *[She pulls a handkerchief from her purse, lifts her eyeglasses, and dabs her eyes.]*

LANTANA: Ms. Arbuckle, did you know Michael Nolan prior to this trial?

ARBUCKLE: Yes, of course. Mikey is Edna's nephew—grand-nephew. I've known him all his life. *[She looks at Mikey and begins to cry.]* I can't imagine why he'd do a thing like this. *[sobs]*

[BIRDWELL objects:]

BIRDWELL: Your Honor, I move to strike the witnesses' imaginings from the record.

WHEELHOUSE: Sustained. Jurors will disregard the witnesses' imagination. You may continue, Ms. Lantana.

LANTANA: As Mrs. Buchanan's bookkeeper, did you have any knowledge about her wishes regarding the distribution of her wealth after her passing?

ARBUCKLE: *[sniffs]* Yes, I helped revise her Will every four years, make any changes and what not. We'd just finished updating it early last May. Right before she went up to Louisville for Derby.

LANTANA: Was Michael Nolan included as an heir to any portion of Mrs. Buchanan's estate?

ARBUCKLE: Yes, he was. Mikey was to receive eighty-thousand dollars as his part of the inheritance.

[Murmurs circle throughout the courtroom.]

WHEELHOUSE: *[Lightly taps his fly swatter]* Quiet please.

LANTANA: No further questions, Your Honor.

[LANTANA moves to her place at the Prosecutor's table.]

WHEELHOUSE: Would the Defense like to question the witness?

BIRDWELL: *[stands]* Yes, Your Honor. *[Approaches the witness]* Good afternoon, Ms. Arbuckle.

ARBUCKLE: Afternoon.

BIRDWELL: Aside from bookkeeping, do you have other skills or other sources of income?

ARBUCKLE: Yes. I douse for water, for people needing to dig a well. And I read palms.

BIRDWELL: A palm reader. Did you ever read Mrs. Buchanan's palms?

ARBUCKLE: No. She didn't believe in stuff like that. I don't think she even knew that her husband Wilbur's ghost was haunting their horse barn.

BIRDWELL: So, you see ghost. Can you see the future?

ARBUCKLE: No, but I've had premonitions.

BIRDWELL: Did you have a premonition regarding Mrs. Buchanan's untimely demise?

ARBUCKLE: I had a dream about her, after she passed.

BIRDWELL: You don't say? And what was she doing in your dream?

ARBUCKLE: She was floating down Stoner Creek, on an inner tube. She seemed to be searching for something.

BIRDWELL: Did your dream reveal what she was searching for?

ARBUCKLE: Well, in my dream she wasn't wearing her hat. She always wore a hat—in public—she was very self-conscious about her... *(whispers)* bald spot.

BIRDWELL: Did you say *bald* spot?

    [LANTANA stands.]

LANTANA: Relevance?

BIRDWELL: I'll move on, Judge. Ms. Arbuckle, you've testified you've known Mr. Nolan all his life. Was he a good boy?

ARBUCKLE: I thought he was. I don't know where he went wrong.

BIRDWELL: *[Turns to the judge]* Judge, could you kindly remind Ms. Arbuckle that my client is innocent until proven, beyond a reasonable doubt, otherwise.

WHEELHOUSE: Ms. Arbuckle. Do you understand that Mr. Nolan only stands *accused* of murder?

ARBUCKLE: I understand. I hope it ain't so. Rest her soul.

BIRDWELL: Thank you. Now, do you know anything about a banjo that once belonged to Mrs. Buchanan?

ARBUCKLE: Yes. It was Wilbur's, Edna's late husband. After he passed, Edna gave it to Mikey.

> *[BIRDWELL goes to the evidence table and picks up the banjo again. He holds it forth for Ms. Arbuckle to examine.]*

BIRDWELL: Is this the banjo that was given to Mikey Nolan by Mrs. Buchanan?

> *[ARBUCKLE adjusts her eyeglasses and squints at the instrument.]*

ARBUCKLE: It is, I think. It might be.

BIRDWELL: So, you're not sure?

ARBUCKLE: I only know she gave him one a few years back.

BIRDWELL: *[turns toward the judge]* No further questions, Your Honor.

> *[BIRDWELL returns to his seat at the Defense table.]*

WHEELHOUSE: Ms. Arbuckle, you are dismissed.

[ARBUCKLE stands and exits.]

WHEELHOUSE: Does the State have additional witnesses to call?

LANTANA: No, Your Honor.

WHEELHOUSE: Very well. This concludes Day One of this trial. I remind the Jurors to refrain from discussing this case with anyone. We will reconvene tomorrow at 10 am. Court is dismissed.

[WHEELHOUSE strikes his gavel twice.]

POTTER: All rise.

[WHEELHOUSE stands and exits.]

(Lights out.)

INTERMISSION

ACT 2 / DAY 2

BOURBON COUNTY COURTHOUSE - PARIS KENTUCKY - AUGUST 13TH, 1974

(Lights up on:)

> *[NOLAN, BIRDWELL, LANTANA and
> JURORS are seated in their respective places.
> POTTER is standing to address the Court.]*

POTTER: All Rise. The Honorable Franklin Wheelhouse presiding.

> *[WHEELHOUSE enters and takes his place at
> the bench.]*

WHEELHOUSE: You may be seated. Good morning one and all. Today is August the 13th 1974 and it is Day 2 in the trial of Kentucky vs. Michael P. Nolan. The Defense may call its first witness.

BIRDWELL: Thank you, Your Honor. The Defense calls Mr. Elbert Pace to the stand.

> *[PACE enters to be sworn in.]*

POTTER: Please raise your right hand. *[PACE raises his hand.]* Do you swear that the testimony you are about to give is the truth, the whole truth and nothing but the truth, so help you God?

PACE: I swear. I do.

POTTER: Please be seated.

[PACE sits and runs his fingers through his hair.]

BIRDWELL: Would you please state your name for the Court and tell us your occupation.

PACE: Yes. Elbert Pace. I'm a barber here in Paris.

BIRDWELL: Did you cut my hair the day before yesterday?

PACE: You know I did.

BIRDWELL: And did you powder my wig?

PACE: *[chuckles]* It's not a service I normally offer but—yep, I gave it a smart dose of talc.

BIRDWELL: Did we talk about this case and what questions you may be asked in Court today?

PACE: We talked a spell. Was that a 'no-no'?

BIRDWELL: No, no. It was not a 'no-no.' I just want the jury to know that a witness is entitled to know what to expect in Court. So, you were prepared, some might say coached by me, regarding your testimony?

PACE: I guess you might call it that.

BIRDWELL: So, now that we all know what we need to know, I'll ask if you knew the late Mrs. Edna Buchanan.

PACE: Of course. Everybody knew her.

[LANTANA stands.]

LANTANA: Your Honor, I move to strike the witnesses' answer. "Everybody" is speculative.

WHEELHOUSE: Sustained. Mr. Pace, could you be more specific as to your personal knowledge of Mrs. Buchanan and leave the rest of us out of it?

PACE: Sorry, Frank. I mean, your highness. Yes, I knew Edna Buchanan.

BIRDWELL: What were your feelings toward Mrs. Buchanan?

PACE: Come again?

BIRDWELL: Did you like her?

PACE: *[laughs]* Nobody liked... er, I mean... No, I did not particularly care for Mrs. Buchanan. She's raised my rent every year for the past fifteen.

BIRDWELL: So, she was your Landlady. Did she own the building where you cut hair?

PACE: Mine and every other building in town. The ones she didn't own, she was tryin' to buy.

BIRDWELL: What word would you use to best describe Mrs. Buchanan?

PACE: First word that comes to mind might insult the mother of my coon dogs. I'll just say the old lady was greedy.

[LANTANA stands.]

LANTANA: Objection Your Honor! Mrs. Buchanan is not on trial here, and I'll not have her character besmirched.

BIRDWELL: Judge, no besmirchin' intended. I'm merely trying to establish that the deceased was not well liked in the community and therefore, there could have been other folks, aside from my client, that may have had an itch to end her life.

WHEELHOUSE: Mr. Birdwell, the Sheriff's department, and KDCI sorted out all the suspects months ago. The District Attorney of Bourbon County has examined their findings and has brought charges against a single individual, your client, the defendant: Mr. Nolan. I will sustain the prosecutor's objection and ask that you leave Mrs. Buchanan's character out of it.

[BIRDWELL nods, acknowledging the Judge's reprimand.]

BIRDWELL: Mr. Pace, putting Mrs. Buchanan's character aside, did you witness the aftermath of her fall from the roof?

PACE: It haunts me, Horace. I won't soon forget it.

BIRDWELL: How did you come upon the scene?

PACE: I had just locked up the barbershop and was headed home. At the corner of 8th as I was about to cross, I looked to my right. That's when I saw the body, Mrs. Buchanan... on the sidewalk. It was fairly gruesome.

BIRDWELL: What else do you remember?

PACE: A pickup truck, pulling away from the curb.

BIRDWELL: Do you know whose truck that was?

PACE: Yep, Billy Miller's red '62 Ford.

BIRDWELL: Do you recall any other details?

PACE: I noticed a hubcap laying on the curb near the body.

[From the evidence table, BIRDWELL picks up a hubcap.]

BIRDWELL: Judge, if it pleases the Court, the Defense would like to enter this item as exhibit H-01.

WHEELHOUSE: Duly noted.

BIRDWELL: *[to Pace]* Is this the hubcap you saw near Mrs. Buchanan's body?

PACE: Looks like it.

[BIRDWELL, still holding the hubcap, picks up the banjo from the table. He holds them side-by-side for comparison.]

BIRDWELL: Can you point out the similarities between this hubcap and this banjo?

PACE: Well, to my ear, if you lose a hubcap, it makes 'bout same racket as a banjer. *[laughs]*

BIRDWELL: What about their shapes and sizes?

PACE: Well, the bottom part of that banjer is round like the hubcap. They're about the same size.

BIRDWELL: *[to Pace:]* Much obliged, Bert. *[to Wheelhouse:]* No more questions, Your Honor.

> *[BIRDWELL returns the hubcap and banjo to the evidence table and retakes his seat beside the defendant.]*

WHEELHOUSE: Ms. Lantana, would you care to cross-examine this witness?

LANTANA: Yes, Your Honor.

> *[LANTANA stands and moves toward the witness stand.]*

LANTANA: Good morning, Mr. Pace.

PACE: Morning, ma'am.

LANTANA: You seem to have a keen memory. Are you sure you saw *[points] that* hubcap at the scene?

PACE: That's the hubcap - or one just like it.

LANTANA: What happened next - after Mr. Miller's truck sped away?

PACE: Next thing I saw was Cookie coming out of his burger joint.

LANTANA: Was there an exchange between you and the restauranteur?

PACE: Who?

LANTANA: Ravi Kochar, the owner of the hamburger stand. Did the two of you speak?

PACE: Cookie was talkin' a blue streak in his native tongue. I don't have a clue what he was saying.

LANTANA: Did either of you call for help?

PACE: Cookie rushed back inside his place. I saw him through the window—on the phone. It wasn't long 'fore the ambulance and Darryl showed up.

LANTANA: Deputy Miles?

PACE: Yep. He told me I should go ahead and get home.

LANTANA: Mr. Pace. Are you sometimes called to local funeral parlors to care for the hair of deceased persons?

PACE: Yes, I offer that service. I like doing it. The customers never complain! *[laughs]*

LANTANA: Were you called to attend to Mrs. Buchanan's hair after her death?

PACE: No, ma'am. No need. I heard they ended up doing a closed casket.

LANTANA: Thank you, Mr. Pace. *[She turns to the bench.]* No further questions, Your Honor.

WHEELHOUSE: You may step down, Mr. Pace.

> *[PACE leaves the witness stand. LANTANA takes her seat.]*

WHEELHOUSE: You may call your next witness, Mr. Birdwell.

BIRDWELL: The Defense calls Vincent Carney to the stand.

> *[CARNEY, a slender young man in Mechanics coveralls takes the stand.]*

POTTER: Raise your right hand. *[CARNEY complies.]* Do you swear that the testimony you are about to give is the truth, the whole truth and nothing but the truth?

CARNEY: Yes, sir.

POTTER: Please take a seat.

[BIRDWELL approaches the witness.]

BIRDWELL: Good afternoon, Mr. Carney. Could you state your name and occupation for the Court?

CARNEY: Vincent Carney. I work at Wiley's Tires on Main Street.

BIRDWELL: Do you also have another part-time occupation?

CARNEY: I play fiddle with the String Busters.

BIRDWELL: Can you tell us about the day the band filmed a performance on the roof of the Beacon Building?

CARNEY: It didn't end well.

BIRDWELL: No, it did not. Besides the filming with the band, was there *something else* you personally were trying to accomplish that afternoon?

CARNEY: That didn't go well either.

BIRDWELL: Is that *something else* something you confessed to Detective Frick during his interro... your interview with him?

CARNEY: Yeah...

BIRDWELL: Go ahead, it's fine to talk about it. The defendant is not pressing charges.

CARNEY: I had a plan to steal Mikey's banjo that day.

BIRDWELL: Why would you want to do that? Wasn't Mikey a good friend?

CARNEY: He still is. He's not one to hold a grudge.

[NOLAN gives an enthusiastic 'thumbs up.']

NOLAN: Ten-four Good Buddy!

WHEELHOUSE: *[slaps his flyswatter]* Mr. Nolan. I warned you yesterday. You will not speak unless spoken to. Understood?

NOLAN: *[less enthusiastically]* Ten-four, Judge.

BIRDWELL: Mr. Carney, what was it about Mr. Nolan's banjo—that made you decide to steal it?

[LANTANA stands.]

LANTANA: Objection Your Honor. Relevance?

WHEELHOUSE: Mr. Birdwell?

BIRDWELL: I'm gettin' to it, Judge. I guarantee to establish relevance.

WHEELHOUSE: Objection overruled. You may continue.

BIRDWELL: *[to Carney]* So, why *did* you decide to steal Mr. Nolan's banjo?

CARNEY: The money. I'd heard Mikey's banjo was pretty rare. It once belonged to a guy named Joel Sweeney. Guess he was pretty famous back in the day. Somehow, Mrs. Buchanan's husband ended up with it. Not sure Old Man Buchanan ever learned to play it but after he died, Mrs. B. gave the banjo to Mikey.

BIRDWELL: How did you learn that the banjo was valuable?

CARNEY: I found out talkin' with Reggie Rose, the luthier in Lexington.

BIRDWELL: For the Court, can you tell us what a luthier does?

CARNEY: Somebody that makes and repairs instruments —like banjos and guitars. He's worked on my fiddle a few times.

BIRDWELL: Did Mr. Rose tell you what he thought Mikey's banjo might be worth?

CARNEY: He said as much as three thousand bucks—to the right buyer.

BIRDWELL: Really? Was Mr. Rose an interested buyer?

CARNEY: We never talked about who might buy it.

BIRDWELL: We? Who's we? You and Mr. Rose?

CARNEY: No, no. Mr. Rose had nothing to do with it. Me and Billy.

BIRDWELL: Billy Miller? Mrs. Buchanan's hired hand?

CARNEY: Yep. Billy agreed to help swipe the banjo for fifty bucks. We decided to do it the day of the filming on the roof.

BIRDWELL: Weren't you afraid that stealing Mikey's banjo might affect your friendship, maybe even break up the band?

CARNEY: *[laughs]* I didn't plan on getting caught.

BIRDWELL: And you didn't get caught—but you did confess—isn't that right?

CARNEY: Yep. When the Detective interviewed me, I spilt the beans.

BIRDWELL: What was Detective Frick's reaction when you told him that you had stolen Mikey's banjo?

CARNEY: Seemed like he didn't give a damn. Thought I was making it all up.

[LANTANA slowly rises.]

LANTANA: Objection. The witness cannot know the thoughts of Detective Frick.

WHEELHOUSE: Sustained.

BIRDWELL: Weren't you able to prove to the detective that you had stolen Mr. Nolan's banjo?

CARNEY: Nope. On account we lost it. It bounced out of the back of Billy's truck at the bridge. We both went back to look for it but figured it got washed somewhere down the creek.

> *[Again, BIRDWELL picks up the banjo from the evidence table. He holds it forth for Carney to examine.]*

BIRDWELL: So, someone must have found it. Isn't this it?

CARNEY: *[Laughs]* No, that's the prop banjo—the one Mikey had planned to smash. It was perfect for our decoy. I switched it with Mikey's good one—put it in his case. You know, so when he picked it up, the weight of his banjo case would be like—normal.

BIRDWELL: Where did the prop banjo come from?

CARNEY: Not sure, I think it was Greg's.

BIRDWELL: Did he purchase it through the Sears Catalogue Store?

CARNEY: Could of. It looked fairly new. Beats me.

> *[**LUNGREN**'s chair suddenly rolls out from under her, and she hits the floor. NOLAN rises to help her, but she jumps up quickly and re-seats herself as if nothing happened.]*

BIRDWELL: Do you know Beverly Frick, who works at the catalogue store?

CARNEY: Sure. I know her.

BIRDWELL: Would you consider Beverly a friend?

CARNEY: You might say that. *[Flashes a wicked smile toward the Jurors]* She's pretty friendly.

BIRDWELL: Did Mrs. Frick come up to the roof when you all were filming?

CARNEY: I think she came up a couple of times, to have a smoke and check out what we were doing.

BIRDWELL: Was she present when Mrs. Buchanan fell?

CARNEY: *[pauses, thinks]* Maybe. After the scream, things went kinda bonkers. For sure it was me, Sam, and Mikey. Sonja had left, I think... Beverly... coulda been, but I can't really remember.

BIRDWELL: Thank you, Mr. Carney. No further questions.

WHEELHOUSE: Would you like to cross-examine this witness, Ms. Lantana?

LANTANA: Yes, Your Honor.

> *[LANTANA clears her throat as she approaches the witness.]*

LANTANA: Mr. Carney. Isn't this whole story—about stealing Mr. Nolan's banjo—something you and Mr. Miller just made up to help the defendant in this case?

CARNEY: No ma'am. It happened. We stole Mikey's banjo.

LANTANA: Did you see Mrs. Buchanan fall from the roof of the Beacon Building?

CARNEY: No, ma'am. My back was to the ledge. I couldn't see Billy or the sidewalk. I was down on one knee tryin' to make it look like I was just puttin' my fiddle away. But the whole time, I was reelin' out more of the extension cord to lower Mikey's banjo down to Billy.

LANTANA: So, let's get this straight. The banjo you claim to have been stealing was tied to an extension cord. Is that your testimony?

CARNEY: Yes'um, a long one. Billy was waitin' down on the sidewalk near where he'd parked on 8th.

LANTANA: If you could not see Billy Miller, how do you know he was waiting below or even if he received the alleged stolen banjo?

CARNEY: We'd worked it out. Billy whistled like a bluejay once'd he was in place. that was my signal to start lowering Mikey's banjo down to him.

LANTANA: Mr. Carney, did you hear Ms. Buchanan scream when she fell?

CARNEY: I thought I heard Billy scream.

LANTANA: Are you sure the scream did not come from Ms. Buchanan?

CARNEY: I'm not sure. I thought it was Billy.

LANTANA: Did you ever look over the ledge of the roof?

CARNEY: After the scream, I stood up and peeked over the wall. I seen Mrs. Buchanan down on the sidewalk. Billy jumped in his truck and pulled off. Mikey's banjo, the nice one, was in the bed of Billy's truck, on top of the hay.

LANTANA: Did the police - Officer Miles, collect the alleged extension cord?

CARNEY: No, ma'am. I tossed it before he showed up.

LANTANA: So, you admit you tampered with potential evidence?

CARNEY: If you say so. I tried to tell Detective Dic— Frick—

[LANTANA cuts him off.]

LANTANA: That's all, Mr. Carney. *[turns to the judge]* No further questions, Your Honor.

WHEELHOUSE: You are dismissed, Mr. Carney.

[CARNEY stands and exits. LANTANA returns to her seat.]

WHEELHOUSE: Mr. Birdwell, you may call your next witness.

BIRDWELL: The Defense calls Sonja Garcia to the stand.

[GARCIA, a modestly dressed young woman, steps forward to be sworn in.]

POTTER: Please raise your right hand. *[GARCIA raises her hand.]* Do you swear that the testimony you are about to give is the truth, the whole truth and nothing but the truth, so help you God?

GARCIA: I swear.

POTTER: Please be seated.

BIRDWELL: Good afternoon. Could you please state your name and occupation for the Court?

GARCIA: Sonja Garcia. I work at Millersburg Muffins. It's a bakery.

BIRDWELL: Are you a baker?

GARCIA: And a candlestick maker.

BIRDWELL: *[laughs]* You're pulling my leg.

GARCIA: No sir. We also sell candles shaped like muffins. They're scented to smell like blueberries, cranberries, and pumpkin spice. We also do little skulls for El Dia de los Muertos—Day of the Dead.

BIRDWELL: Oh, I've not seen the skull candles, but I do remember the muffin ones from around Christmas time. Ms. Garcia, what is your relationship to the defendant?

GARCIA: We're not related. We were dating. Then we broke up. But now we're back together. Unless he goes to prison that is.

> *[GARCIA looks toward Nolan and silently mouths, "Sorry."]*

BIRDWELL: Are you a member of the Bourbon String Busters band?

GARCIA: Yes. I play mandolin. When I can. When I'm not at the bakery.

BIRDWELL: Ms. Garcia, did you see Mrs. Buchanan fall or, otherwise, be pushed or knocked off the roof of the Beacon Building?

GARCIA: No, I'd already started downstairs. After I'd given Mikey a piece of my mind.

BIRDWELL: Are you referring to the argument you had with Mikey? The one you told Detective Frick about?

GARCIA: Yeah, I was breaking up with him. It got pretty heated. We weren't paying much attention to the old lady.

> *[LANTANA raises a hand.]*

LANTANA: Objection, Judge. Would you please advise the young lady not to refer to the victim as an old lady?

WHEELHOUSE: Ms. Garcia, please refer to the victim as 'the deceased' or Mrs. Buchanan. Ms. Lantana, please refer to the witness as Ms. Garcia—not a *young* lady. You may continue Mr. Birdwell.

BIRDWELL: Was Mr. Nolan holding his banjo during your argument?

GARCIA: No. I think he'd already put it away, in its case.

BIRDWELL: Who had the prop banjo? The one Mikey was supposed to smash?

GARCIA: I don't know anything about that.

BIRDWELL: What were you and Mr. Nolan arguing about?

GARCIA: I heard he'd been 'two-timing' me.

BIRDWELL: Cheating on you? With whom?

GARCIA: Can I say?

BIRDWELL: You may.

GARCIA: I heard that Mikey had been stepping out with Beverly Frick.

BIRDWELL: Did you know that Beverly is related to Detective Eugene Frick?

GARCIA: Yeah, they're married.

BIRDWELL: But this alleged affair was only a rumor, correct?

GARCIA: Well, it's not a complete rumor; Beverly has been known to mess around.

> *[**LUNGREN** types furiously—super focused on the conversation.]*

BIRDWELL: Did you ever *confirm* that she was messing around with the defendant, your boyfriend, Mr. Nolan?

> *[GARCIA shoots a look in Nolan's direction. NOLAN drops his head to avoid eye contact.]*

GARCIA: Guess I'll never know for sure. Mikey and I were already into it when Beverly came up to the roof for a smoke.

BIRDWELL: Beverly Frick was on the roof that day?

GARCIA: Yes.

BIRDWELL: Did you confront her about her alleged involvement with Mr. Nolan.

GARCIA: No. I just split.

BIRDWELL: Meaning, you left the roof?

GARCIA: I didn't want it to come to fisticuffs.

BIRDWELL: *[Turns to the bench]* No further questions Your Honor.

[BIRDWELL returns to the Defense table.]

WHEELHOUSE: Would the State like to cross-examine the witness?

LANTANA: Yes, Your Honor. *[approaches the witness]* Ms. Garcia, in your interview with Detective Frick, did he ask about an alleged affair between his wife and Mr. Nolan?

GARCIA: Nope. He never mentioned it.

LANTANA: But you *did* tell Detective Frick that Mr. Nolan loved his banjo *more* than he loved you. Correct?

GARCIA: I was still sore at Mikey. Like I said, we've made up since.

LANTANA: Of course. Now, do you know where and how Mr. Nolan got his treasured banjo?

GARCIA: It was a gift from Mrs. Buchanan.

LANTANA: Do you know *why* she gave him the instrument?

GARCIA: No, not really. They're family. Guess she didn't need it.

LANTANA: Aside from the gift of the banjo, are you aware that Michael P. Nolan is also named as a beneficiary in the Last Will and Testament of the late Mrs. Buchanan?

GARCIA: I didn't know that, not then. I heard that later, on the news.

LANTANA: Isn't it true that Mr. Nolan had plans for the money he was set to receive upon Mrs. Buchanan's death?

GARCIA: Not sure, for a while he talked about wanting a tour bus. So, the band could travel to out-of-state gigs and bluegrass festivals. Not sure that's in the cards now.

LANTANA: Did you ever encourage your boyfriend, Mr. Nolan, to cause Mrs. Buchanan's death?

GARCIA: What?

LANTANA: Or conspire with him to kill her?

GARCIA: Of course not. The nerve! No!

LANTANA: No further questions.

WHEELHOUSE: You may step down Ms. Garcia.

[GARCIA stands and exits.]

WHEELHOUSE: The Defense may call its next witness.

BIRDWELL: Your Honor, the Defense calls William Miller to the stand.

[MILLER, a wiry young man in an ill-fitting sport coat with his hair slicked to one side, enters and comes forward to be sworn in.]

POTTER: Please raise your right hand. *[MILLER does so.]* Do you swear that the testimony you are about to give is the truth, the whole truth and nothing but the truth, so help you God?

MILLER: Yes, sir.

POTTER: Take a seat.

[BIRDWELL approaches.]

BIRDWELL: Good morning. Could you please state your name for the Court?

MILLER: William Miller. My friends call me Billy.

BIRDWELL: Thank you, Billy. Were you employed by the late Mrs. Buchanan?

MILLER: Not a full-time thing. I just helped out at her place from time to time. Mowin', paintin,' fixin' fences—stuff like that.

BIRDWELL: So, you worked part-time as a 'Hired Hand'?

MILLER: Yes, sir. Mrs. B.'d usually pay me a few bucks. Sometimes give me lunch.

BIRDWELL: Were you running an errand for Mrs. Buchanan on the afternoon of March 16th?

MILLER: Yes, sir. She'd ask me to fetch a few bales of hay from Ferguson's. They still had some of their winter stock.

BIRDWELL: Was your pickup truck parked near the Beacon Building that afternoon?

MILLER: I stopped there. Went over to grab a Coke at Cookie's.

BIRDWELL: Were you aware that Mrs. Buchanan was in town that afternoon?

MILLER: No, sir. No idea.

BIRDWELL: Did you see her fall from the top of the Beacon Building?

MILLER: Heck yeah. She nearly landed smack on top of me.

BIRDWELL: Why were you there, at that spot, at that time? It wasn't just to have a soft drink, was it?

MILLER: I had fetched the hay for Mrs. B., and I *was* thirsty, but I was sippin' the Coke mostly to kill time. Waitin' for Vinny to lower Mikey's banjo down.

BIRDWELL: Vincent Carney?

MILLER: Yes sir, the fiddler.

BIRDWELL: We've heard in earlier testimony that Mrs. Buchanan's scalp bore marks made by a banjo; from having been struck with the instrument. Do you know how that happened?

MILLER: Sure do. Got yer pocket watch?

> *[BIRDWELL removes his watch from his vest pocket and hands it to MILLER.]*

MILLER: Got Mrs. B.?

BIRDWELL: This should suffice.

> *[BIRDWELL pulls a Barbie doll from his coat pocket and turns to the judge.]*

BIRDWELL: With the Court's permission, Your Honor. This is for demonstration purposes only. It's on loan from my granddaughter. And *yes*, Mr. Miller and I rehearsed this visual demonstration prior to his taking the stand.

WHEELHOUSE: *[Considers the props. Addresses the prosecutor.]* Ms. Lantana, do you have any objection to a demonstration by this witness using these items?

LANTANA: *[Sighs]* None at this point, Your Honor.

WHEELHOUSE: *[To Birdwell]* You may proceed.

BIRDWELL: Thank you, Your Honor. *[BIRDWELL hands the Barbie to Miller.]* Go ahead, Billy. Show the Court what you saw.

MILLER: Alrighty. *[With his right hand, MILLER holds the pocket watch by its chain.]* Let's say this here is

Mikey's banjo on the extension cord. *[With his left hand, he lifts the Barbie high above his head.]* And this here is Mrs. Buchanan—'cept she wasn't wearing a swimsuit. The banjo was swingin' back and forth like this. *[He demonstrates causing the pocket watch to move like a pendulum.]* When it was 'bout halfway down to me— that's when Mrs. B. come off the roof. The banjo swang in her direction—and bam! *[The pocket watch makes contact with the Barbie's head.]* Clocked her right on the noggin'—then she hit the deck!

> *[For emphasis, MILLER whacks the Barbie against the railing of the witness stand. The doll's head pops off.]*

MILLER: *[whispers]* Oops.

> *[MILLER hands the watch and headless Barbie back to BIRDWELL.]*

BIRDWELL: Thank you, Mr. Miller. No further questions, Your Honor.

> *[BIRDWELL retrieves Barbie's head from the floor, pockets the doll and his watch then returns to his seat beside Nolan. NOLAN gives him a pat on the back.]*

WHEELHOUSE: Would the State like to question the witness?

> *[LANTANA stands.]*

LANTANA: Indeed, Your Honor. *[Approaches the witness...]* Good afternoon Mr. Miller.

MILLER: My friends call me Billy.

LANTANA: Mr. Miller, did you try to render any aide to Mrs. Buchanan after she fell?

MILLER: Render?

LANTANA: Did you try to help her? Perform resuscitation or first aide of any kind?

MILLER: A lotta good that would'a done. She was a goner.

LANTANA: Why didn't you stay at the scene, or call for help? Don't you think that would have been the right thing to do?

MILLER: I was worried I'd get caught with Mikey's banjo. Reckon I panicked. Once I cut the banjo loose from the 'stension cord, I tossed it in with the hay, then hightailed it outta there.

LANTANA: So, what became of this stolen banjo? Did you and Mr. Carney sell it?

MILLER: No ma'am. I lost it. It must of bounced out of the bed of my truck when I hit that big pothole right at the bridge leaving town—you know the one.

LANTANA: Mr. Miller, are you aware that the Defense, in order to create even further confusion, has suggested that the injuries on Mrs. Buchanan's scalp could have also been inflicted by a hubcap?

[BIRDWELL stands.]

BIRDWELL: Objection! The Defense was merely putting forth an alternate theory.

WHEELHOUSE: Attorneys, please approach the bench.

[LANTANA and BIRDWELL approach and 'sidebar' with the judge. Meanwhile, MILLER leaves the witness stand and goes to the evidence table. He picks up the hubcap.]

MILLER: Hey, this is my hubcap!

[WHEELHOUSE, LANTANA and BIRDWELL turn in unison toward Miller.]

WHEELHOUSE: Son, put down the evidence and return to the witness stand.

[MILLER quickly does as he's told.]

MILLER: Sorry sir.

[The 'sidebar' concludes. BIRDWELL returns to his seat at the Defense table. LANTANA stands awaiting the judge's decision.]

WHEELHOUSE: The objection is sustained. Ms. Lantana, please do not speculate on the tactics of the Defense.

LANTANA: *[Turns to Miller]* Mr. Miller, do you believe a swinging banjo contributed to Mrs. Buchanan's death?

MILLER: *[Chuckles]* Pretty sure it was the sidewalk.

LANTANA: Mr. Miller, let me put it this way: Do you know what initiated her fall?

MILLER: Did what?

LANTANA: Her fall. What caused it?

MILLER: Maybe she just... fell.

LANTANA: Fell? Over a wall, specifically put there to prevent people from falling off the roof?

MILLER: It is sort of a *low* wall. She could'a jumped. I had an uncle once—

[LANTANA interrupts aggressively.]

LANTANA: Mr. Miller! Isn't it true that this entire story about you and Vincent Carney trying to steal Mr. Nolan's banjo is just a tall tale cooked up to save Mr. Nolan from paying for his crime?

MILLER: No ma'am. That's what happened.

LANTANA: *[Calmly turning to the judge]* No further questions, Your Honor.

WHEELHOUSE: You may step down, son.

MILLER: *[points to the evidence table]* Can I take my hubcap?

WHEELHOUSE: You may not. You are dismissed.

> *[MILLER sheepishly leaves the stand and exits.]*

WHEELHOUSE: You may call your next witness Mr. Birdwell.

BIRDWELL: Your Honor, the Defense would like to *recall* Detective Eugene Frick back to the stand.

> *[LANTANA stands.]*

LANTANA: May I approach the bench your honor?

WHEELHOUSE: Yes, with Mr. Birdwell please.

> *[LANTANA and BIRDWELL approach the bench and exchange whispers in another sidebar with the judge. After a brief exchange, WHEELHOUSE gestures for both attorneys to take their respective seats.]*

WHEELHOUSE: Seems Detective Frick is not presently in the courthouse. We'll take a recess for lunch while we locate the detective then resume testimony thereafter. The Court is in recess until 1:30. Jurors, your lunch will be served shortly.

> *[WHEELHOUSE raps his gavel and exits back to his chambers.]*

POTTER: All rise.

> *[ALL rise. POTTER opens the door for the JURORS exit. LANTANA gathers her papers. POTTER approaches Nolan.]*

POTTER: Let's go Mr. Nolan. The jail has your lunch waiting.

NOLAN: Oh boy. Beenie Weenies.

BIRDWELL: Bon Appetit Mikey. See you after lunch.

> *[POTTER escorts NOLAN out. A middle-aged woman dressed in business attire (ALICE RHODES) rushes into the courtroom eager to speak with Birdwell.]*

BIRDWELL: Alice? What are you doing here? Did you lock up the office?

RHODES: They found it!

BIRDWELL: Really? Where?

RHODES: Hank Jenkins fished it out of Stoner Creek.

BIRDWELL: Get it down here. But wrap it up in a blanket or something. I'd like to surprise Detective Frick *after* he takes the stand.

(lights down slowly)

(lights up on:)

> *[ALL are back in Court seated.]*

POTTER: All rise.

> *[Everyone stands. WHEELHOUSE enters and takes the bench.]*

WHEELHOUSE: Mr. Birdwell, you may now call your next witness.

> *[BIRDWELL stands.]*

BIRDWELL: Thank you, Your Honor. The Defense _recalls_ Detective Eugene Frick to the stand.

[Hot and bothered, FRICK enters through the double doors at the back of the courtroom. He is not dressed for Court, more likely the golf course.]

WHEELHOUSE: Detective Frick, you are still under oath. Please take the stand.

[FRICK complies. BIRDWELL approaches...]

BIRDWELL: So sorry to interrupt your golf game, Detective, but I felt it necessary to ask you back to the witness stand to answer a few additional questions.

FRICK: Shoot.

BIRDWELL: That wasn't a question. But this is: Did you carry out some surveillance, at the Beacon Building prior to the tragic incident of Mrs. Buchanan's death?

FRICK: Surveillance? Prior... Could you be more specific?

BIRDWELL: Sure. Did you have reason to keep an eye on your wife, at her place of employment, *prior* to Mrs. Buchanan's death?

FRICK: Not sure what you're implying, I often park on the street out front—to wait for Beverly to get off work.

*[**LUNGREN** seems less enamored with Frick than she was on Day One.]*

BIRDWELL: On the night of Tuesday February 19th—it was cold and rainy if you recall—did you see a man inside the catalog store speaking to your wife?

FRICK: Folks come and go. I saw people.

BIRDWELL: On that night, did you happen to see a male customer engaged in a passionate kiss with your wife?

FRICK: No.

BIRDWELL: Do you *recall* seeing a man with a banjo leave the store?

FRICK: During the *brief* time I was parked, I saw a lady with her child leave the store with merchandise... and one man. Can't say what their items were. It was dark outside.

BIRDWELL: Is it *possible* that the man was carrying a banjo?

FRICK: Could have been.

BIRDWELL: Did you recognize that man?

FRICK: He'd pulled the hood up on his raincoat. I didn't get a good look at his face.

BIRDWELL: But did you have any idea... who it was?

FRICK: I'm pretty sure I know who it was.

BIRDWELL: And who do you think it was?

FRICK: *[pause]* I plead the fifth.

BIRDWELL: It's good to see the detective knows his Constitutional rights. Let me ask you this, are you a jealous husband?

[LANTANA stands.]

LANTANA: Objection. Relevance?

BIRDWELL: Your Honor, I will prove relevance.

WHEELHOUSE: Overruled. You may continue Mr. Birdwell.

[LANTANA sits.]

BIRDWELL: So, are you? A jealous husband?

FRICK: I'm a faithful husband.

BIRDWELL: Prior to this case, were you familiar with any of the musicians who played in the band with Mr. Nolan?

FRICK: Bluegrass ain't my thing. Too twangy. I prefer Country Rock.

BIRDWELL: *[chuckles]* I didn't ask for your taste in music sir. I asked if you were familiar with the musicians who call themselves the Bourbon String Busters. Are you?

FRICK: It's a small town. I'm pretty familiar with who does what.

BIRDWELL: And since it's been brought up, did you and your wife Beverly ever discuss the rumors circulating, in this small town, of her alleged affair with Mr. Nolan?

FRICK: *[Through clenched teeth]* I investigated it. Turned out that was just gossip.

BIRDWELL: Isn't that why you arrived early outside your wife's place of employment on February 19th? To surveil her? To see if you might catch her playing patty-cake with Mr. Nolan?

FRICK: No. I was early because I had finished work early. I wasn't about to drive home—then turn back around to come down and pick up Beverly.

BIRDWELL: If I told you that the man who pulled up his rain hood, whom you've declined to identify, <u>was</u> carrying a banjo, would you have any reason to disagree?

FRICK: No.

> *[BIRDWELL goes back to the Defense table, reaches beneath it, and pulls out a sizable object wrapped in an old quilt. He approaches FRICK while slowly unwrapping the item. It's a banjo—covered in mud and creek scum.]*

> *[Gasps rise throughout the courtroom.]*

BIRDWELL: Fished out of Stoner Creek this morning! Mr. Nolan's ban—

[WHEELHOUSE bangs his gavel repeatedly.]

WHEELHOUSE: That instrument has not been disclosed prior to this trial! It's not allowed, Mr. Birdwell. It is *not* evidence in this case!

BIRDWELL: Your Honor, this is not the *last* **banjo in Paris**. On that table yonder—

[LANTANA jumps to her feet and interrupts.]

LANTANA: Objection! Mr. Birdwell is deliberately misleading the jury!

WHEELHOUSE: Your objection is sustained. The second banjo will not be allowed into evidence. Horace, put it away!

> *[BIRDWELL wraps the banjo back in the quilt and returns it from view beneath the Defense table.]*

WHEELHOUSE: *[addresses the Jurors]* Ladies and gentlemen of the jury. You must disregard the fact that a second banjo has appeared in this courtroom. It is *not* evidence in this case. *[Turns to Birdwell]* Do you have any further questions for Detective Frick Mr. Birdwell?

BIRDWELL: No sir. Nothing further.

WHEELHOUSE: *[Sighs heavily]* The State may now question the witness.

LANTANA: Thank you. *[approaches the detective]* Detective Frick—first, let me apologize for the inconvenience of having you return to the witness stand. However, I'm pleased that you're here and I will take this opportunity to ask you a few questions. If I may?

> *[FRICK nods.]*

LANTANA: Detective Frick, are *you* on trial here?

FRICK: No, ma'am.

LANTANA: Who *is* on trial?

FRICK: Michael P. Nolan. For the murder of Mrs. Edna Buchanan.

LANTANA: Precisely. And as a result of your investigation, are you convinced that the defendant committed the crime?

FRICK: I have no doubts.

LANTANA: Thank you, Detective. No further questions, Your Honor.

WHEELHOUSE: Detective Frick, you may step down.

> *[FRICK leaves the stand and makes his way toward the aisle to exit...]*

WHEELHOUSE: You may call your next witness, Mr. Birdwell.

BIRDWELL: The Defense calls... Mrs. Beverly Frick to the stand.

> *[Whispers buzz throughout the gallery as BEVERLY FRICK, a buxom brunette wearing high heels and a mini skirt, enters the courtroom. She passes her husband as he moves up the aisle toward the exit. The detective avoids eye contact with her as she continues to the witness stand.]*

POTTER: Please raise your right hand. *[B. FRICK complies.]* Do you swear to tell the truth, the whole truth and nothing but the truth, so help you God?

B. FRICK: I do.

POTTER: Please be seated.

> *[**LUNGREN**'s expression reveals she dislikes Beverly. (Perhaps some past history?)]*

BIRDWELL: Good afternoon, Mrs. Frick.

B. FRICK: Afternoon.

BIRDWELL: Could you please tell the Court where you work?

B. FRICK: I work for Sears & Roebuck on the corner of eight and Main.

BIRDWELL: On the first floor of the Beacon Building?

B. FRICK: Yes, in the catalog department.

BIRDWELL: Did you hear about the rumors that were circulating? About you having an affair?

B. FRICK: Oh, I heard. It wasn't all rumor. But it wasn't *all* true.

> *[DETECTIVE FRICK bursts back into the courtroom, his face red with rage.]*

FRICK: *[Shouts]* Honey! You don't have to answer that!

WHEELHOUSE: *[Strikes his gavel twice.]* Detective. Pipe down. I'll allow you to remain, but you must take a seat. Mr. Birdwell, you may continue.

> *[BIRDWELL keeps an eye on the detective until he complies with the judge's instructions.]*

BIRDWELL: Thank you, Judge. Mrs. Frick, to clarify, did you just state that the rumored affair was not a rumor?

B. FRICK: I did.

FRICK: Bev! Please!

WHEELHOUSE: Detective Frick! You *will* remain silent, or I will have you removed.

B. FRICK: I need to answer, Eugene! These people deserve to know!

FRICK: *[Stands]* It's over, Bev. Hear me? It's over!

B. FRICK: It's *been* over, baby. For a *long* time!

> *[Heads turn as DETECTIVE FRICK stomps out of the courtroom.]*

WHEELHOUSE: Mr. Birdwell, you may continue.

BIRDWELL: Thank you, Judge. Mrs. Frick, to reiterate, the rumored affair, involving you, was not a rumor, correct?

B. FRICK: Correct.

BIRDWELL: So, the man your husband saw leaving your store with a banjo, is he the man you were romantically involved with?

B. FRICK: *[Smiles]* Yes, sir. He's the one.

BIRDWELL: And the banjo? Did he have a banjo the night your husband saw him?

B. FRICK: That banjo wasn't his. It was a catalogue order. He was picking it up for a friend. He had a claim check.

BIRDWELL: As a tadpole in law school, I was taught from day one never to ask a question that I didn't already know the answer to. But, in this case—if you are willing—could you please name the man you kissed, the one who left the store with a banjo on the rainy night of February 19th?

B. FRICK: It was... Billy. Billy Miller.

> *[Gasps and giggles trickle throughout the courtroom. WHEELHOUSE taps his gavel. Everyone hushes.]*

BIRDWELL: Billy Miller? Not the defendant Mr. Nolan?

B. FRICK: Mikey's cool and all, but Billy's got it goin' on... if you know what I mean.

BIRDWELL: I think I do.

[BIRDWELL turns to the judge.]

BIRDWELL: Your Honor. I move that this trial be dismissed on the grounds that the Detective in the case was prejudiced by his belief that his wife was having an affair with a banjo player, the man he mistook for Mr. Nolan. My client was unjustly targeted for a crime he did not commit.

[LANTANA stands.]

LANTANA: Objection! Mr. and Mrs. Frick's marital friction has no bearing on this case whatsoever, Your Honor.

WHEELHOUSE: I'll ask both attorneys to meet me in my chambers. This Court will stand in recess until we iron this out.

[WHEELHOUSE lowers his gavel.]

POTTER: All Rise.

[All Rise. WHEELHOUSE exits to his chambers. BIRDWELL and LANTANA follow him. BEVERLY FRICK remains on the stand somewhat confused.]

BIRDWELL, LANTANA & WHEELHOUSE: *[Ad Lib: Indistinct yelling and arguing off stage.]*

[B. FRICK is still on the stand. LANTANA and BIRDWELL enter from the judge's chambers followed by WHEELHOUSE.]

POTTER: All Rise.

[EVERYONE stands. WHEELHOUSE takes his seat behind the Bench and addresses the Court.]

WHEELHOUSE: You may be seated. *[ALL sit]* I apologize for the delay in this trial, but it fell upon me to consider the motion, from the Defense, that this case be dismissed *with* prejudice *due* to prejudice. After conferring with both attorneys in my chambers, I have decided to delay my ruling on the matter until *all* witnesses have been called and questioned. Mr. Birdwell, do you have any further questions for Mrs. Frick?

BIRDWELL: Yes. Just a few. Thank you, Your Honor.

> *[BIRDWELL rises and addresses the witness.]*

BIRDWELL: Mrs. Frick, did you come up to the rooftop of the building where you work on the day the band was filming?

B. FRICK: I *was* curious about what they were doing— but that's where I usually take my smoke breaks.

BIRDWELL: Were you on the roof when Mrs. Buchanan fell?

B. FRICK: No. I was only there for a minute or two. I had to get back to work.

> *[BIRDWELL turns to the bench.]*

BIRDWELL: No further questions Your Honor.

> *[BIRDWELL returns to his seat at the Defense Table.]*

WHEELHOUSE: *[addresses Ms. Lantana]* Would the Prosecution like to cross-examine this witness?

LANTANA: No, Your Honor, the Prosecution is only interested in facts. We have no desire to further drag Mrs. Frick through the mud of sordid rumors and innuendo.

WHEELHOUSE: So be it. Mrs. Frick, thank you for your testimony. You are free to go.

> *[B. FRICK rises, adjusts her miniskirt, leaves the stand, and exits up the aisle and through the main courtroom doors.]*

WHEELHOUSE: Mr. Birdwell, does the Defense have any additional witnesses?

BIRDWELL: Only one Your Honor. The defendant, Michael Paul Nolan.

WHEELHOUSE: You may proceed.

> *[BIRDWELL gestures for Nolan to rise and take the stand. NOLAN stands and comes forward.]*

POTTER: Please raise your right hand. *[NOLAN complies]* Do you swear to tell the truth, the whole truth and nothing but the truth, so help you God?

NOLAN: I swear.

BIRDWELL: *[Approaches NOLAN]* Has anyone forced or coerced you to take the stand today in your own defense?

NOLAN: No sir.

BIRDWELL: Did anyone advise you that it's usually a *bad* idea for the defendant to testify at his own trial?

NOLAN: *You* did.

BIRDWELL: But after reminding you of your Fifth Amendment right to remain silent, you still decided to bear witness on your own behalf, correct?

NOLAN: Yes. I thought it best.

BIRDWELL: Okay, well let's get to it. Mr. Nolan, did you love your great-aunt?

NOLAN: With all my heart. She never did me nothing but good.

BIRDWELL: It is my understanding that you have a very different version of events that took place on the day your great-aunt Edna died, correct?

NOLAN: Yes sir. I haven't said a word about it to nobody.

BIRDWELL: Not even Detective Eugene Frick?

NOLAN: When he interviewed me, I told him it was just an accident. That a breeze had blown Aunt Edna's hat off her head... That she'd reached to grab it, tripped on the extension cord, and fell off the roof.

BIRDWELL: But that wasn't true, was it?

NOLAN: No sir.

*[**LUNGREN** types furiously.]*

BIRDWELL: In giving false statements to Detective Frick, were you trying to protect someone?

NOLAN: Yes.

BIRDWELL: And who is that someone you were trying to protect?

NOLAN: Beverly... Frick.

[Gasps rise throughout the courtroom.]

BIRDWELL: So, are you now admitting to being involved romantically with Mrs. Frick?

NOLAN: Guess everyone's figured that's true by now. Funny she said it was Billy but... who knows. Maybe she had a thing with him too. It was just that, sitting across from Bev's husband at the police station didn't seem like the best time to confess that I'd been fooling 'round with his wife.

BIRDWELL: Is there another reason you were trying to protect Mrs. Frick?

NOLAN: Yeah, because she did it. She killed Aunt Edna.

*[The stenograph falls off Lungren's tiny desk. A rumble of chatter fills the courtroom. **LUNGREN** quickly fetches the stenograph and regains her composure. WHEELHOUSE strikes his gavel.]*

WHEELHOUSE: Order please. Order!

BIRDWELL: Why would Mrs. Frick do such a thing? What did she have against Mrs. Buchanan?

NOLAN: For one, she despised her. I think that gave her the guts to do it... but that's not *why* she did it.

BIRDWELL: Wait, back up, why did she despise her?

NOLAN: Said she was the worst customer she'd ever dealt with. Said Aunt Edna tried to get her fired... more than once.

BIRDWELL: But that's not why, you are now alleging, she killed her?

NOLAN: No. See, thing is, I was tired of playing just Bluegrass. I mean, don't get me wrong, I dig Bluegrass... but the minute I dropped the needle on "Dark Side of the Moon" I knew I wanted to switch things up.

BIRDWELL: What about the moon?

NOLAN: It's an album. Pink... ah.. a rock band. Anyway, Beverly was stoked that I wanted to take my music in a new direction. She got the big idea that I might have what it takes to become a Rock star. She got really excited when I mentioned maybe moving out to California.

BIRDWELL: So, did Mrs. Frick want to help you pursue that California dream?

LANTANA: Objection. Counsel is putting words in his mouth.

WHEELHOUSE: I'll allow the question. I'd like to hear what the defendant has to say.

BIRDWELL: Did Mrs. Frick want to help you pursue your dream?

NOLAN: Somehow, she got it in her head that we would run off *together*. But that was never... *my* plan.

BIRDWELL: But Beverly Frick *was* aware that you stood to inherit a good deal of money from your great aunt's estate... on her passing? Correct?

NOLAN: *[exhales]* Yeah. Wish I had never mentioned the inheritance to her.

BIRDWELL: Did Mrs. Frick believe that amount of money could get the two of you to California and kickstart your Rock music ambitions?

NOLAN: I had no idea that she was planning to kill Aunt Edna. She *had* talked about leaving her husband... different ways we might run off together... but killing was never part of it.

BIRDWELL: So, you're saying she took matters into her own hands?

NOLAN: Yes sir. She did.

BIRDWELL: But you were willing to take the fall for her crime?

NOLAN: No. No, I was just hoping everybody would believe it was an accident. Once I got charged with the murder, I knew I'd have to take the stand to get my side of the story out. By the way, I don't think I was the only one trying to protect Beverly.

BIRDWELL: Go ahead, who else?

NOLAN: Her old man. I don't think he pinned this on me just because he was jealous. I think Detective Frick knows she did it.

[Hushed conversation fills the room.]

BIRDWELL: Is there anything else you'd like to add, Mr. Nolan?

NOLAN: No. That about does it, I guess.

BIRDWELL: Your Honor, in light of Mr. Nolan's testimony, I make my second motion for a mistrial!

[BIRDWELL returns to his seat at the Defense table.]

WHEELHOUSE: Not so fast, Horace. Ms. Lantana, would you care to cross-examine the witness?

[LANTANA rises.]

LANTANA: Absolutely, I would, Your Honor.

[LANTANA approaches Nolan.]

LANTANA: Mr. Nolan. Do you think you can just make up a story on the witness stand and 'poof'—get yourself acquitted?

NOLAN: I told the truth. Beverly killed Aunt Edna. I saw her do it.

LANTANA: You did? Then tell us... please tell us *exactly* what you saw.

NOLAN: Well, likes been said, Sonja and I were arguing. *By the way, we are back together now.* Anyway, we were deep into it when Beverly came up to the roof. When Sonja saw Bev, she stormed off down the stairs. Aunt Edna was over by Sammy watching the sunset, but she turned round and started toward us. She told Bev, "You need to stay away from my nephew." That's when Beverly shoved her—hard. Aunt Edna stumbled backwards, tripped over the extension cord, and went over the wall.

LANTANA: If all that *actually* happened, why didn't the other boys see it? Or tell anyone about it?

NOLAN: I'm the only one who saw Beverly shove Aunt Edna. Nobody turned around until Billy screamed.

LANTANA: But weren't they curious about the spat you were having with Ms. Garcia, or the words of warning Mrs. Buchanan spoke to Mrs. Frick?

NOLAN: Maybe, but see, it's band code that we don't meddle in each other's personal business.

> *[LANTANA shakes her head in disbelief as she strolls to the Evidence Table and picks up the banjo.]*

LANTANA: Mr. Nolan, given Mrs. Frick is *not* accused of this crime, and you are the *only* defendant in this case, I'd like to get back to the facts.

WHEELHOUSE: A question please?

LANTANA: *[to Nolan]* Didn't you use *this* banjo, the so-called 'prop' banjo, to kill your great-aunt, Edna Buchanan?

NOLAN: No, ma'am. I did not.

LANTANA: Did you use the banjo Mrs. Buchanan gave you as a murder weapon?

NOLAN: No, ma'am. I did not.

LANTANA: I will remind you that you are under oath Mr. Nolan. Do you understand that?

NOLAN: Yes, ma'am. I do.

LANTANA: Did either of the two banjos in question come in contact with Mrs. Buchanan's head?

NOLAN: You heard what Billy said, with the Barbie.

LANTANA: What do YOU say?

NOLAN: Seems something hit her head. I'll go with the hubcap.

> *[BIRDWELL stifles a chuckle as a smattering of laughter ripples throughout the gallery.]*

LANTANA: Did you conspire with *anyone* to carry out the murder of your Aunt Edna, to speed up the process of gaining your inheritance from her estate?

NOLAN: No. Beverly did all the conspiring.

LANTANA: Do you plan to use your inheritance to go to California and make it big as a Rock Star?

NOLAN: Guess that depends on the verdict.

LANTANA: And again, how much do you expect to receive from your late, great Aunt Edna Buchanan's estate?

NOLAN: Eighty something.

LANTANA: Eighty thousand dollars.

NOLAN: Is that a question?

LANTANA: Let's get this straight. You're saying, that up until today, you mentioned to no one that you saw Beverly Frick shove Mrs. Buchanan to her death? And you expect the Jurors to believe that?

NOLAN: *[looks to the Jurors]* I sure hope they do. It *is* the truth.

LANTANA: We'll hear from the Jurors soon enough. No further questions, Your Honor.

[LANTANA returns to her seat.]

WHEELHOUSE: Mr. Birdwell, would you care to redirect?

BIRDWELL: No, sir. I'm done.

WHEELHOUSE: Is Mr. Nolan your final witness?

BIRDWELL: He is, Your Honor.

WHEELHOUSE: Mr. Nolan, you may step down.

[NOLAN leaves the witness stand and takes his seat beside Birdwell.]

WHEELHOUSE: *[to all]* Having heard all testimony and evidence presented in this trial, it is my decision that the two motions to dismiss this case be denied. The case *will* proceed to Jury Deliberation.

Therefore, closing arguments from both attorneys will be heard. But before that, it is my duty to instruct the Jurors regarding *what* should be considered in order to reach a verdict. *[Turns toward Jurors]* Please pay close attention to the instructions I am about to read to you...

> *[WHEELHOUSE reads from prepared text*
> *waving his flyswatter to punctuate his cadence:]*

WHEELHOUSE: Michael P. Nolan, the defendant in this case, has been accused of the crime of First-Degree Murder. Although the defendant waived his fundamental right *not* to testify in his own trial, you must not be influenced in any way from the fact that he took the stand. His testimony must be weighed by the same criteria as any other witness testimony. Also, the lawyers are not on trial. Your feelings about them should not influence your decision in this case.

> *[In unison, LANTANA and BIRDWELL look to*
> *each other with a nod and a wink.]*

WHEELHOUSE: Whatever verdict you render must be unanimous. The verdict of the jury must also be in writing. Therefore, a verdict *form* will be provided for you. which reads as follows:

> *[WHEELHOUSE shuffles papers to find the*
> *verdict form.]*

WHEELHOUSE: ... if I can find it. *[more paper shuffling... He finds it]* Here we go. Once you've reached a unanimous verdict, you will check only *one* of the boxes here; A, B, C or D. *[pause]*

A: The Defendant is Guilty of First Degree Murder.

B: The defendant is guilty of Second Degree Murder.

C: The defendant is guilty of Manslaughter. Or...

D: The Defendant is Not Guilty.

After the attorneys deliver their closing arguments, *[Looks to Potter]* Bailiff Potter, will escort you back to the Jury Room. There, you will be asked to choose a Foreman, a man or woman, who will preside over your deliberations. It is also the Foreman's job to sign and date the Verdict Form when *all* of you have agreed on a verdict. After which, the verdict form will be handed to me for the reading of the verdict. Thank you for your attention regarding these instructions.

The State will now be asked to deliver its Closing Argument. After which, the Defense will do the same. Ms. Lantana, are you ready to proceed?

LANTANA: Yes, Your Honor.

WHEELHOUSE: Mr. Birdwell, is the Defense prepared to proceed?

BIRDWELL: We are, Your Honor.

WHEELHOUSE: Great. On with the show. Ms. Lantana.

> *[LANTANA takes a deep breath*
> *and approaches the podium facing*
> *the JURORS.]*

LANTANA: Thank you, Judge Wheelhouse. Thank you, ladies, and gentlemen of the Jury. The State's burden in this case, my burden, is to prove *with facts* that Michael P. Nolan murdered Mrs. Edna Buchanan. *[Looks over her shoulder to BIRDWELL]* The Defense wants you to doubt those facts. Mr. Birdwell wants you to believe Mr. Nolan's testimony and ignore the facts. *[pause]* I'll ask you to pardon the pun, but... don't fall for it.

Mr. Birdwell's entire strategy in this case has been to confuse you. And he knows that he only needs to confuse *one* of you to gain an acquittal. Don't fall for it.

There's been lot of talk about *this* banjo or *that* banjo, the tale of two banjos. However, the State does not have a burden to prove what weapon, if any, was used to kill Mrs. Buchanan.

> *[LANTANA holds up the oversized photo of the smiling Mrs. Buchanan that she used in her opening statement.]*

LANTANA: Edna Buchanan did not have any children or grandchildren. But she did have one great-nephew whom she bragged about and showered with her generosity. Little did she know that her goodwill would be repaid with violence... motivated by greed.

The evidence has shown that this generous woman was killed because Michael P. Nolan could not wait to receive his portion of her estate. That being said, I'd like to remind you that it is also not the State's burden to prove motive. Our sole burden is to prove that Mr. Nolan's actions were the cause of Mrs. Buchanan's death.

> *[LANTANA puts away the photograph.]*

LANTANA: Why was the bluegrass band filming on top of the Beacon Building? Was it merely a *cool* idea to imitate the antics of Britain's Fab Four? No! Michael Nolan chose the location, well in advance, as a stage for murder. A place where an accidental fall was quite probable. And, though *none* of Mr. Nolan's bandmates confessed knowledge of his murderous scheme, I appeal to you to not take their testimony at face value. Individually, each one of them had reasons to protect their friend. Yes, Michael Nolan had a motive: Money. And opportunity: a three-story rooftop. And means: A weapon. He killed his great-aunt then tried to cover it up with a tall tale and a little help from his friends.

In Mr. Birdwell's attempts to confuse you, he also included the false accusation of misconduct by the State's Lead Detective and further stirred up that confusion with hearsay about illicit love affairs. Don't be swayed by the legal slight-of-hand that the Defense has tried to dazzle you with. Don't believe the defendant's outrageous attempt to pin this murder on Mrs. Frick. Believe the facts, not the fiction. Don't fall for it. Thank You.

[LANTANA returns to her seat.]

WHEELHOUSE: Mr. Birdwell, you may address the jury.

[BIRDWELL stands and goes to the podium before the Jurors. **LUNGREN** *cracks her knuckles and takes a deep breath.]*

BIRDWELL: Good afternoon, ladies and gentlemen. *[gestures to Ms. Lantana]* As Ms. Lantana has already stated, the Prosecution has the *sole* burden of proof in this case. We, the Defense, are under *no* obligation to prove *anything*.

Though the State wants to sway you to believe otherwise, the defendant did not murder Mrs. Buchanan. In fact, it's astonishing that the Prosecution had no clue coming into this trial about what really happened. Mrs. Buchanan did not die due to a blow from a banjo wielded by her great-nephew. As Mr. Nolan has testified, it was Beverly Frick who thought the best path to win his love and gain her 'happily ever after' was to push Mrs. Buchanan off the roof of the Beacon Building.

[BIRDWELL reveals and displays an enlarged photo of Mrs. Buchanan similar to the one shown by the State but, this copy has been altered to resemble a jigsaw puzzle with pieces missing .]

BIRDWELL: And because the State *desperately* wants you to believe their version of the story, they've *deliberately* left things out of the picture. They've held back some crucial pieces of the puzzle.

*[BIRDWELL sets the puzzle photo at the base
of the podium facing the JURORS.]*

BIRDWELL: To start with, they never doubted even *one* conclusion from Detective Frick. Nor the fact that he never questioned Mr. Nolan about the affair with his wife, who by the way, lied through her lipstick while on the witness stand.

There were no questions from the Prosecution about the Detective's refusal to believe Billy Miller and Vincent Carney after they openly confessed to being partners in their attempt to steal Mr. Nolan's prized banjo. All missing pieces.

Eugene Frick not only suppressed information obtained through witness interviews, he also botched the evidence when he transferred Mrs. Buchanan's blood onto the banjo that was taken into evidence. There are more than a *few* things Detective Frick *failed* to detect. Did he know about his own wife's alleged involvement in this crime? More missing pieces, folks.

They've declared 'premeditation' without a *shred* of evidence yet based their entire case on the cliche' motive of money. Facts are missing, folks!

Never once did the State mention Michael Nolan's love and deep affection for his Aunt Edna. Where is that piece? I could go on...

*[BIRDWELL picks up the puzzle photo again
and holds it high for all to see.]*

BIRDWELL: Every fact they've left out in their case against Mr. Nolan are missing pieces that they want *you* to ignore. When things are missing, doubts *should* arise. The missing pieces in this case—a case which should have never been concocted from the get-go, much less brought to trial—should convince you beyond *all doubt* that Michael P. Nolan did not kill Edna Buchanan. These doubts can only lead to *one* conclusion: A verdict of NOT GUILTY! And lastly, please remember that the eyes of those who have gone before us are watching. *[smiles]* I thank you kindly.

> *[BIRDWELL bows and his wig falls off. He retrieves it then returns to the Defense table and sits. NOLAN gives him a congratulatory shoulder punch.]*

WHEELHOUSE: Jurors, we have come to the conclusion of this trial. The verdict in this case is now in your hands. You are hereby dismissed to begin your deliberations. The Court will stand in recess until a verdict has been reached.

> *[WHEELHOUSE lifts his flyswatter, see his mistake, picks up his gavel and strikes it twice.]*

POTTER: All rise.

> *[ALL Rise. POTTER opens a door for the Jurors; JURORS exit. WHEELHOUSE exits to his chambers. POTTER moves to the Defense table and escorts NOLAN out. LANTANA and BIRDWELL gather their papers and start toward the main aisle. BIRDWELL offers his opponent a 'Ladies first' gesture. LANTANA and BIRDWELL exit.*
> ***LUNGREN*** *stands and picks up her Stenograph. Exhausted, she slowly exits...]*

(The stage stands empty. The Lights shift gradually to a bluish hue.)

> *[A Royal Ascot hat trimmed in red rises from behind the judge's bench followed by The GHOST of Edna Buchanan. The hat settles onto her head.]*

BUCHANAN: BOO! Yes, I'm the ghost of the late Mrs. Edna Buchanan. *[picks up and strikes the judge's gavel]* Please be seated.

[BUCHANAN moves with a hitch in her step toward the evidence table where she stops and retrieves her left shoe. She moves to the Defense table, leans against it, and puts on the shoe then addresses the audience:]

BUCHANAN: Before ya'll scoot out to wait for the verdict, I've got a few things I'd like to clear up. Yep, I'm here to testify! Like prissy Miss Lantana said in her openin' statement, this is *my* story—so, who better to tell it than me?

[She drifts over to the witness stand.]

BUCHANAN: So happens, not every witness who takes the stand tells the truth. Surprise, surprise. As for me, being deceased and all, I got nothing to lose by tellin' the truth, the whole truth and nothing but the truth, *[raises her right hand]* so help me God.

[She sits and continues...]

BUCHANAN: Did folks around town despise me? Generally speakin', yes—but I never gave a rat's ass what people thought. Was I murdered? Yes. With a banjo? Not exactly. The boys' testimony about trying to steal Mikey's banjo, as crazy as it seems, is true.

The blow from the banjo was just the way Billy told it with Swimsuit Barbie. It struck me on my way down. However, a pothole did not cause the banjo to bounce out of his truck. Once Billy heard Mikey had been arrested for killing me, he got worried that he'd be caught with the murder weapon so, he tossed the banjo into Stoner Creek.

Old man Birdwell nearly flipped his wig when that second banjo was fished out of the drink. Somehow, he thought he'd just found the key that would exonerate Mikey. By the way, as clever as Birdwell thinks he is, that old fool is just a simple-minded country lawyer who sees Atticus Finch every morning when he looks into the mirror.

[She pulls a flask from her bra, uncaps it, and takes a big swig.]

BUCHANAN: Bourbon County's finest! What can I say. When I'm sober, I'm cantankerous and ornery. Which is the way most folks usually saw me in the light of day. But a good dose of bourbon always set me in a better mood. My mood was good the day my life ended.

Did Mikey have a motive for my murder—like Ms. Lantana laid out? His inheritance? Well, I won't argue that he didn't. See, 'bout a year ago, Mikey stopped by to ask me for a loan—said he was thinkin' 'bout movin' out west. I was sober and cranky at the time. I laughed in his face and told him to stop dreamin'. A week or so later, after three too many Mint Juleps, I had a change of heart, so to speak... Needless to say, I don't always make the best decisions when I've been drinkin'. But I did decide to have pity and leave Mikey somethin' in my Will, for later I thought, a nice little 'nest egg' to use once some years had pulled his head out of the clouds.

[She takes another swig of the Bourbon.]

BUCHANAN: Was old man Birdwell right about police misconduct? The blood on *that* banjo yonder, *[points toward the evidence table] was* indeed just sloppiness on Detective Frick's part, like Birdwell laid out. Frick may come off as a jerk, but he's actually a pretty good detective. He's just a lousy husband. Frick was way too wrapped up in his work to give Beverly the attention she needed. No wonder she's been 'steppin' out' on him. Yes, it *was* Mikey that came out of the catalogue store on that rainy, slobbery night. And yes, Mikey *was* carryin' a banjo—cause he never left home without it. Beverly wasn't merely cheatin' on her husband, she had fallen madly in love with Mikey and yes, wanted to be part of his California dream.

How do I know all this? That's one of the benefits that comes from being dead. I can move around as I please now. Even walk through walls. Listen in on people's conversations. By the way, Annabelle was right about Wilbur's ghost. He *is* hauntin' our horse barn. But back to the afternoon I died;

Before I went ass over teakettle off the roof, I'd had my usual few, *[holds up flask]* and was actually enjoyin' watchin' the kids film their little show.

As they were wrappin' things up, I was standing over by the Welles boy, gazin' out at the glorious sunset, until— *drum roll please...* Beverly Frick showed up. That's when I stepped over to ask her *kindly* to keep her affections away from Mikey. Then it happened, Bev got in my face and pushed me! I stumbled backwards, my shoe caught that extension cord and I fell to my death. The scream folks heard? That was Billy and me both screaming at the same instant. Me fallin', him squallin'. Meanwhile, Beverly was hightailin' it down the stairs.

Turns out, Annabelle had let the cat out of the bag about my intentions to name Mikey in my Will. Once Mikey told Beverly about his future inheritance*, it was* Beverly alone who began plottin' my demise. I suppose money, mingled with delusions of grandeur, can be powerful persuaders. Was her shove premeditated, or was it just a knee-jerk reaction to my warnin' to stay away from Mikey? That, I'm not clear on... but I will tell you that Mikey *never* conspired with Beverly to kill me.

You might ask why I don't just drift back to the jury room and make the truth known to all of 'em? Can you imagine Judge Wheelhouse's face if the Jury told him they'd been visited by the ghost of the deceased durin' their deliberations? *[laughs]* That would be grounds for a mistrial for sure.

For my sake, I do hope the Jurors get this right. If not, I

might be destined to haunt this courthouse forevermore. *[Hears offstage footsteps]* Speaking of the jury, here they come...

> *[BUCHANAN'S GHOST exits from whence she came.]*

(Lights back to normal as:)

> *[POTTER enters with NOLAN and BIRDWELL and escorts them to the Defense table where they remain standing. LANTANA enters and stands at the prosecutor's table.]*

POTTER: All rise.

> *[All others stand or remain standing as the judge enters. POTTER crosses and opens door for Jurors to enter. Jurors enter. The FOREPERSON has the Verdict Form in hand. Jurors take their places in the jury box but remain standing.]*

WHEELHOUSE: You may be seated. *[ALL sit]* Has the jury reached a verdict?

POTTER: Yes, Your Honor.

WHEELHOUSE: *[to the FOREPERSON]* If you'd please hand the verdict form to Bailiff Potter.

> *[The FOREPERSON hands the verdict form to POTTER. POTTER gives it to WHEELHOUSE.]*

WHEELHOUSE: Mr. Nolan, please stand for the reading of the verdict.

> *[NOLAN and BIRDWELL stand. WHEELHOUSE Reads:]*

WHEELHOUSE: In the case of The Commonwealth of Kentucky vs. Michael P. Nolan for the crime of First-Degree Murder of Mrs. Edna Buchanan: We the jury find the defendant...

[Suddenly, the main doors of the courtroom fly open...]

MILES [O.S. shouts]: Wait! Judge! Hold up!

[ALL turn as DEPUTY MILES enters with BEVERLY FRICK in handcuffs. Her face is streaked with mascara from crying.]

MILES: Your Honor, Sorry for bustin' in—but I need to inform the Court that I've got crucial evidence in this case that simply cannot wait!

WHEELHOUSE: *[pause]* This is highly irregular procedure, Deputy, but I'll allow it.

MILES: *[to Beverly]* Go ahead, ma'am. Tell Judge Wheelhouse what you told me.

B. FRICK: *[shouts]* I did it, Judge! I pushed the old biddy off the roof. And I ain't sorry for it!

[The courtroom erupts with chaotic chatter. WHEELHOUSE raps his gavel.]

WHEELHOUSE: Order. Order. Officer Miles, please take Mrs. Frick to the County Jail for further questioning...

[MILES leads B. Frick toward the side door exit (stage right)...]

WHEELHOUSE: ... and find Detective Frick!

MILES: Yes sir, Judge!

B. FRICK: *[As she's being taken out, FRICK throws her cuffed hands up gesturing with pinkies and forefingers extended and shouts...]* Rock on Mikey! I'll always love you!

[NOLAN acknowledges Beverly's shout out with a casual wave of his hand as MILES and B. FRICK exit. NOLAN continues waving broader to get the attention of Judge Wheelhouse.]

WHEELHOUSE: Yes, Mr. Nolan?

NOLAN: Am I free to go now? You know, since Bev just confessed?

WHEELHOUSE: No. You are not. *[Takes a deep breath and exhales heavily.]* Regardless of Mrs. Frick's surprise appearance and apparent confession, it remains my duty to read the verdict as reached by *these* Jurors in the case that is *currently* before this Court.

> *[NOLAN shrugs. He and BIRDWELL remain standing.]*

WHEELHOUSE: Take two... *[Clears his throat; reads:]* In the case of The Commonwealth of Kentucky vs. Michael P. Nolan for the crime of First-Degree Murder of Mrs. Edna Buchanan: We the jury find the defendant...

["Guilty" or "Not guilty" of 1st Degree Murder, 2nd Degree Murder or Manslaughter depending on the volunteer Juror's written verdict.]

*(If the verdict is **GUILTY**:)*

WHEELHOUSE: Guilty. Bailiff Potter, please take Mr. Nolan into custody. Sentencing will be set for Monday, September 23rd. Jurors, I thank you for your service. You are dismissed. *[pause]* Court is adjourned.

> *[WHEELHOUSE strikes his gavel and exits. POTTER opens door for Jurors to exit then crosses to escort Nolan out. BIRDWELL and LANTANA shake hands and exit.]*

(Lights out.)

(Stage lighting that cast shadows of prison bars up on:)

> *[The final tableau for the curtain call: NOLAN sits alone with his banjo playing "My Old*

Kentucky Home." Remaining Cast Members enter from stage left and right to take their bows. The cast members part to reveal NOLAN as he finishes the tune then smashes his banjo.]

(However, *if the verdict is* **NOT GUILTY:)**

WHEELHOUSE: Not Guilty. Mr. Nolan, you are free to go. Jurors, I thank you for your service. Bailiff Potter, please see them out.

[POTTER moves to and opens the door for the Jurors to exit. JURORS begin filing out.]

WHEELHOUSE: Court is adjourned.

[WHEELHOUSE strikes his gavel and exits.]

(Lights out.)

(Rock concert stage lighting up on:)

[The final tableau for the curtain call: NOLAN (sans jacket and tie) 'shreds' "My Old Kentucky Home" on an electric guitar as other CAST MEMBERS enter from the wings to take their bows. NOLAN finishes his solo and smashes the guitar.]

END

ABOUT THE AUTHOR

Last Banjo in Paris is Barry Cook's debut as a playwright, yet he has worked as a professional storyteller for more than forty years.

Barry began making films at age ten and completed his first animated short film, *The Saga of Benny Caru,* before turning fourteen. Self-described simply as a filmmaker, Barry continues his life-long quest to entertain others through his love of stories.

As a director at the Walt Disney Company, Barry directed the short cartoons *Off His Rockers* and *Trail Mix-Up,* as well as Disney's classic animated feature *Mulan.*

For more information about Barry Cook and his work, including his novella *The Happy Place* and its full cast audio play and his children's book *The Gumdrop Ghost,* please visit:

www.StudioPBJ.com